The Academy of Storytelling Presents

Write The Perfect Read

The Fiction Edition

Make Readers Happy While Propelling Them to the Last Page

Kristin N. Spencer

Maria Mountokalaki

For everyone brave enough to write. We see you.

TABLE OF CONTENTS

CHAPTER 1

THE TWO TRIANGLES OF WRITING

What is the first step anyone must take in order to succeed at any endeavor? It might seem like a loaded question, but the answer is annoyingly simple. The first step to success in any industry is always to begin the quest to gain understanding. This approach has been snubbed by creatives all over the globe since the beginning of creation, and writers are no different. There is a group of writers that would have you believe that in order to write a great novel, all you have to do is sit down and let the words flow. But that idealistic approach to writing often leaves new writers (and sometimes even experienced ones) frustrated and ready to hurl their trusty pen (or even laptop) across the room.

People who observe the art world often think, "Well, you either have it or you don't," and while it is true that some people possess more natural talent for specific tasks than others, any skill can be learned if you have enough time. The same is true about drawing, sculpting, film-making, and certainly writing. Just think of the artist slaving away over their canvas for days, weeks, or months. One doesn't just wake up one day and say, "I'm a painter." Even the most amazing painters of our time practice and struggle to learn to properly use their medium. In the case of the writer, their medium is made of vocabulary, grammar, and style. And in the case of their inspiration, it always comes down to one thing: the story.

But what makes a story good or bad or dull or interesting? We all know about concepts like plot, character arcs, and setting, but how do you use these structures to get the reader from the first paragraph of your story to the last page? The answer to this question is far from simple, and the quest to gain understanding is full of distractions and misinformation. That is why you need an experienced guide on your quest (or in this case two guides). This book has been lovingly written to help you, the person who must be a writer (or wants to become one based on the fact that you are reading this book). Though the idea of understanding all the different parts of what makes a story great may seem intimidating, every big machine can be broken down into its tiniest pieces, and that is what we plan to do for you. Once you understand how each piece works, you will be able to construct your own immense story-building machine.

The three main parts of any storytelling endeavor are comprised of character, plot, and setting while the main process involves three different types of people: the writer, the reader, and the book services professional. Because it is simpler to deal with these six topics according to how they are related to each other, we will group them into two different triangles. Together, these two triangles comprise the six pillars of writing.

But I'm Already A Writer

Well then, you are off to a great start. But do you understand *all* of the pieces in your story-building machine? Do you know what the tiniest pieces do? If you want to better understand what makes a character relatable or how the magic of a properly employed setting can cause your plot to race forward, keep reading. There is something new in this book for everyone.

Or maybe you've been writing for years and you're on the verge of quitting. Don't do it! There may be a few parts of your story-building machine that are broken and just need replacing. That doesn't mean you should quit. Look at this book as a second chance to learn to give your stories that something they've been missing. Once you understand how all of the parts fit together, you will be able to channel your passion for writing like never before.

Who Are You?

The pulsing strings of the guitar thump through the recesses of my mind whenever I hear the phrase "Who are you?" Though this melody-evoking utterance is the title of a well-known song, it is also a valid question. Well, there are two of us, so it would probably be best to do one introduction at a time.

Kristin N. Spencer

Hello there, my name is Kristin and I have been in love with books for as long as I can remember. I grew up in sunny (and smoggy) Los Angeles, California. My parents say that as a two- and three-year-old I asked them to read to me constantly. It didn't surprise them when I started to read at four, or when I would spend hours playing the neighborhood librarian in our front yard with piles and piles of colorful books with their worn corners, begging all of the neighborhood children to check out a copy to enjoy. I don't think they ever thought I would make a career out of it, though, even when I announced I had changed my college major for the third time to Comparative World Literature.

Now I spend my days writing my own books while simultaneously working as a developmental editor for my own editing firm, Literary Symmetry. I also run the fabulous Academy of Storytelling, where I teach authors how to understand every intricacy of storytelling (this book is but a taste of all the amazing methods you can learn and employ).

I am also a self-proclaimed geek extraordinaire, a mother to three actual children and two furbabies, the wife of Travis, and a cosplayer. My favorite genres are science fiction and space fantasy while my favorite book has recently changed from *Pride and Prejudice* by Jane Austen to *Star Wars Lost Stars* by Claudia Gray (yes it's that good). But enough about me.

Maria Mountokalaki

Hey everyone, I am Maria, and I was born and raised in the beautiful country of Greece. Ever since I started learning English, way before I began to pursue my career in teaching English to speakers of other languages and then translation, I tried to surround myself with the language. TV shows and movies were my gateway. When I grew up a bit and could afford them, books became my passion. Like a kid in a candy store, I had no idea what genres I'd enjoy or what authors were the best ones. So, I started sampling. My tastes varied from time to time, depending on my current state and interests. Even though this often prevented me from delving deep into a particular genre, it at least made me a book omnivore. At the time of writing this book, my tastes have shifted from fiction to nonfiction, mostly memoirs and books on productivity. I call myself an avid reader, a title I have hung on to even after a three-year reading slump I suffered a little while ago. In fact, I advocate reading so much, that my Master's dissertation was on ways to promote reading for pleasure through educational technologies. Despite my disparate reading tastes, however, as a translator I have and always will prefer to translate fiction.

It is exactly this translating experience that makes me a good copyeditor. After years of handling authors' manuscripts, I have trained my eye to see details that regular readers do not. Shifts in tone, register or cohesion are things I notice in a text because in order to translate I have to read more slowly and carefully than most people. I also have been sort of ruined for relaxed reading because I sometimes find myself wondering how I would translate a specific passage. The positive side effect of this process, however, is that it gives me time to see how different authors develop their stories and what makes some books pleasurable and others just plain awful.

Another thing that defines me as a person is that I'm a proper-linguistic-expression enthusiast or, as some people affectionately call me, a grammar stickler. Like a super hero, I spent years learning to harness this power and use it only for good. I think I have now reached the point when I unleash it only when I'm asked to. If you ever need rescuing, you will find me through Kristin Spencer's editing co-op, Literary Symmetry. Outside of work, people can usually find me watching YouTube videos on productivity and stressing about time management. I also have the best dog in the world. She doesn't know she could do much better, so please don't tell her.

For the purposes of this book, *we* will mostly write as a

collective. However, when needed, we will use *I*, because this book would probably be pretty boring without a few personal stories. It's up to you to determine who the *I* is. Think of it as a fun sort of guessing game.

How To Avoid Wasting Your Potential

Every November, writers from around the world gather at their computers in an attempt to write 50,000 words in one month. From the first-time writer to the experienced sage of words and wisdom, everyone starts out with the dreaded blank page. Their collective goal: to wrestle the first draft of a novel into existence. Every year, people choose one of two camps to join. On one side, planners work meticulously on their outline in September and October. The other side contains those who prefer to write by the seats of their pants, waiting to see what the story will reveal to them as the words come flowing from their mind, through their fingers, and onto the screen (or page). Within forums and on the web we are all encouraged to reserve our judgment. Planning isn't necessarily better than pantsing, right?

Pantsers seem like they're in it for the fun, so we encourage them along. But what I want to know is, is pantsing really all that fun? And at the same time we must examine the argument that espouses that planned writing zaps creativity. Who is right? Is it that every person has to figure out what works for them, or is there a clear winner when it comes to productivity? For that, I think we need to rewind to 2015, my first attempt at writing a novel in 30 days.

I had finally remembered to put the writing time on my calendar after missing it for two years in a row. My efforts were bound to have some return—I knew I would learn something from the experience even if I failed to produce an entire novel. After a few hours perusing through advice on how to tackle this monumental event, I decided that I was a planner. The few scribbled ideas in a notebook were transformed as I added detail after detail into a carefully organized document that would serve as the skeleton for the body of my story. But then it went beyond that. I started to pay attention to the muscles, tendons, and even epidermis. No character or subplot was left unturned. My outline was approximately 7 pages long. *This isn't too long for a 60k book, is it?* The passing thought slid out of my mind as November 1st approached. Every day for thirty days I wrote. And then I realized that after countless days where I started off feeling stuck, my manuscript had ballooned to 99,000 words. But what had happened?

Could it be that planning isn't all that it's made out to be? A few books later, I realized that if I over-planned, there wasn't freedom to see where the book wanted to take me. The way my outlines were constructed changed back to skeletons, and the muscles, tendons, and epidermis revealed themselves as I was writing. But what about pantsing? Could that technique work even better for me?

On a cold and rainy day in Athens, Greece the wind rocked the fabric awning back and forth as I sat down to ponder more about pantsing. The strong scent of wet concrete mixed with the washing away of all the dirt and oil filled my nostrils with its familiarity. The way I saw it, I couldn't even begin to start to write a book without a plan. How would I know when I hit 25% so I could unveil the inciting incident? How would I know how to develop the character arc to achieve a satisfying ending? Would I know by instinct how to deal with those things without planning to? Some writers do, but after a lot of sitting and thinking, walking and thinking, and washing dishes and thinking, I decided that I wasn't that talented. I also remember thinking, *And that's okay.* After that day, I decided to take a permanent position people will no doubt criticize me for: that planning is what a majority of writers need to do if they want to finish a project that doesn't need to be completely rewritten. It's an effort in attaining a quality end product.

Moving forward in this book, I am going to assume that you, my wonderful writer friend, will be planning. Because if you're pantsing, I don't know how I can help you *before* you start writing. As a developmental editor, I can certainly help you *after* you've written if you've decided to only and forever be a pantser, but for the purposes of this book I want to ask you to try (at least once) to plan.

But What If I Don't?

You might be wondering, "What if I don't *what*?" That's a valid question. Think about what will happen if you don't gain the education you need in order to avoid the pitfalls associated with writing a fictional novel. It's important for you to understand that without the right tools at your disposal, you could get caught in a perpetual cycle of uninformed choices that will result in your own discouragement and loss of drive in a realm where you once had nothing but passion. Writer burnout is real, and happens even when experienced writers are utilizing all of their knowledge and understanding. Imagine how common it is for new writers that don't yet grasp all the complexities of their chosen medium. It is our hope that by reading this book, you will avoid the burnout that comes from trying and trying to use the same amateur methods and expecting professional results. Don't we all wish that there were shortcuts in life?

There are no shortcuts when it comes to writing.

However, there are proven methods and time-tested traditions that work. For example, if you're nervous about using a formula for plotting because you feel like it will take all of your creative approaches away, don't worry. Within each system found in this book, there is a ton of room for new ideas and improvisation. Too many people think that if they just keep writing books, they will eventually understand how to write something that will resonate with people, but that isn't true. Education is the cornerstone of a compelling story. Don't trudge through these unknown waters alone.

Get Your Free Worksheets

Before we get into all of the fun details that comprise the magical world of fiction writing, we wanted to give you a free set of printable worksheets that match the different questions we go over later in regard to character, setting, and plot. As a bonus, you'll also be signed up for our helpful emails. We promise not to spam you. Head on over to

https://literarysymmetry.com/wtpr-f/

to download your free worksheets. Now, let's learn how to write fiction, shall we?

CHAPTER 2

The First Triangle: Character, Plot, Setting

After establishing what the six pillars of writing are, let's take a closer look at the first three: the concepts of character, plot, and setting form the internal triangle, the soul of your whole project. No matter how well you handle the second triangle, if your first triangle is not stable, your whole structure will come tumbling down. First you build and furnish a house, and then you have people over. You can't do it the other way around.

When writing nonfiction, the main purpose of a writer is to inform. In the case of fiction, your goal is to entertain. You can still inform your readers, and nonfiction writers can still entertain theirs, but the *main* goal, the reason why you choose to sit at your desk and write away—sometimes missing out on some activities that your non-writer friends might be doing —is to provide people with something that will entertain them. While I don't necessarily mean you should make your audience laugh, it is your job to give them an escape. Stephen King described books as uncommon alchemy you can carry around in your pocket. Who can argue with that? Just think about it. A man writes a description of a place, person, or a creature, and people he has never met can "see" that place, person, or creature years after he wrote it. It's a more complex version of the mind game "try not to think of a pink elephant." In order for you to write compelling fiction, you must think as a reader first. If there is a certain point in your book that you find boring, be sure that this is what your reader will most likely skip. A safe bet is to always write what *you* would like to read. Trust me, you cannot go wrong there. Here's where things get a bit more demanding, though. A successful novel needs to follow certain rules in order to function. This may sound slightly off-putting and counter-creative, but it is true that almost all the novels you have loved followed some steps that made them special to you. This is what the first triangle will help you accomplish.

The Character, Getting Past the First Date

I love examples, so I'm going to use one to explain how strongly I feel about the importance of having a good command of the first three pillars of writing. Let's say you're on a first date with someone. Your goal is to earn their affection, and ultimately, make them invest time in you. How would you talk about yourself in order to make them interested? Would you start off by chronicling every little detail about your life thus far, or would you focus on saying just enough to spark an interesting conversation? Does your date really need to know all about your entire childhood, or can they just hear an interesting anecdote about it? If you bore your date to death, chances are they won't want to go on a second date with you. But if you manage to spark their interest, you might have just gained some more time with them. If later, your relationship blooms, they will be interested to hear about your childhood. If they have started caring about you, it is inevitable that they will want to know what made you who you are. How you got from there to here: this is character.

The Plot, Connecting the Dots

If your life were a novel, how would you describe it in a few words? This seems hard to do, doesn't it? That's because right now you see your life as a whole. But, if you were to only talk about a certain period of your life, wouldn't it be easier? You want to go from point A to point B. You can't just say, "I used to be a bank clerk and one day I decided to become a writer." Instead, you'll give a brief summary of your life up to the point when you realized that you have an interest in the writing craft. Then, you'll mention what drove you to look into it in more detail, what writing courses you attended, how many drafts you threw away, and how hard you worked in order to write something that moved people. See? All this is pretty interesting, and people who want to know you would want to hear it. And their experience will be so much richer if you make them see things from your perspective, feel your pain and then share your joy. At the end of your narration, you'll be left with people who see you in a new light and are glad they took the time to get to know you: this is plot.

The Setting, Don't Overdo It

I was born in the early 80s, a time when the internet was not yet a thing. Video calls only happened in science fiction movies, and shows on-demand were beyond this world. If I am to describe that period of my life to a younger person, someone who can't remember a time they couldn't just look something up the minute they wanted to, I would have to give them a few details to help them understand how life was back then. I wouldn't want to bore them with every detail about that time, though. I could say how much cheaper things were, and give them a specific example like a gallon of gas (or a liter of petrol), but there would be no point in listing the prices of everything. I could say that we had to rent VHS tapes in order to watch a movie, but I wouldn't go into the minute details of how a VCR works. I could also tell them how much simpler the TV news was at the time, but I wouldn't start telling them all of the past events. I would only focus on giving them just enough information to get them acquainted with the time, without overwhelming them: this is setting.

CHAPTER 3

THE SECOND TRIANGLE: THE WRITER, THE READER, AND THE BOOK SERVICES PROVIDER

While the first triangle is based on all the different aspects of writing, the second triangle is based on all of the people involved with the writing process. Without people who will interact with our books, what is the point of writing? "I write for myself," you might say (although I know not many people are in that Emily Dickinsonesque position), but there is still someone interacting with your writing: you as a reader.

Like other forms of art, the creation of a manuscript is only part of the overall experience. First, the artist creates their piece using skill and some sort of medium. Second, the artist usually introduces the piece to a few selected people for feedback. Third, the artist introduces the piece to consumers who are encouraged to interact with the piece and form their own conclusions about it. This three-step process is exactly the same format we see with writing, whether it be fiction, nonfiction, poetry, prose, screenplays, or any of the other family members that comprise the world of the written word. In this book, though we will focus solely on fiction, many of the principles apply to other types of writing as well.

In order to understand the first part of this triangle, we need to take a journey to gaze pensively in the mirror.

The Writer, Professional Imaginator

What is a writer? You may think that the simple definition of this word is someone who takes words, makes thoughts with them, and writes them down. I'm sorry to spoil your notion of what a writer is, but I think the meaning of this six-letter word would be better described with this definition.

writ·er /'rīdər/*noun*
a person who learns all about words, syntax, and diction in order to wrestle some type of written work into submission for the education and/or enjoyment of their fellow humankind at the cost of their worn, wearied, yet invigorated soul.

When I talk to other writers (aspiring writers included, because someone who writes is indeed a writer) they usually ask me what my first step to becoming a writer was. For many years, I described my adventures into professional blogging because it forced me to put out articles every week, and that meant I was constantly writing. But now I realize it started way, way before that. When I was thirteen years old, I attempted to write my first novel about a young girl named Bobby who had to go and stay with family friends over the summer after her parents had gotten themselves into some financial trouble. But why did I do that? Why did I think I could write a book? The answer isn't because someone told me I could or because anyone encouraged me to try. Think back to my bio (this is Kristin writing). My parents said I would demand for them to do what? Read to me all the time. In fact, my parents thought it was okay for me to read the classics when I was quite young. I remember reading *Jane Eyre* at age eleven and thinking *wow!* Because my parents let me read good books, I thought I could write them. How hard could it be? Fast forward over twenty years later, and 33-year-old, first-time novelist me would tell you that writing isn't an easy endeavor.

The most important thing to do if you want to write is to read! It's so important I even broke the current trend of not using exclamation points aside from dialogue. That's how much I want to impress upon you that reading good books is the most important thing you could ever do as a writer. The second most important thing to do is to learn your medium. See, I didn't use an exclamation point there because it's only the second most important thing. Though reading will definitely boost your writing IQ, you also need to study things like vocabulary and grammar so that when you have an idea of what you want to say, you can say it in the cleverest way possible. Clever readers love to read books by clever authors. Don't you?

Now, imagine that you've studied your medium by reading and understanding how to use the tools available to you as a writer and written your story. What is the next step? Remember the process we discussed just a few paragraphs ago? The feedback stage is upon us. But how do we get the feedback we *need* instead of general feedback? Though we will find feedback in the book services stage, we must first consider who it is we do the writing for: it's time to look deeper at the reader.

The Reader, An Elusive Creature In Its Natural Habitat

If you take a tour around my living room, you will find a strange collection of items, but the most prominent theme will be stacks and stacks of completely unrelated books. A mishmash of children's literature, science fiction, nonfiction, contemporary fiction, and fantasy books litter my shelves waiting to be read. They stare at me, donning names on their spines from Judy Blume to Judd Apatow, daring me to read them, and I will. Someday I will read them all (finishing them is a different matter all together). But in order to earn space on one of my someday-shelves a book must pass several book-background checks. You see, I myself am one of the elusive creatures: I am a reader.

It all started when I was just a child, but as I grew up, things started to get way more serious. My parents weren't thrilled when I changed my major from art, to business economics to comparative world literature. But the last one stuck. That's right, I got a Bachelor's which I equate to a fancy degree in reading. I consider myself to be a professional reader. Though some days you might find me reading in the pursuit of education instead of mere entertainment, I always consider reading a pleasure: until it's not.

This year has been particularly heart-breaking for me. I stopped reading more books than I finished, and I couldn't help but wonder why. If you're going to insist it's because I've turned into a book snob, I assure you that isn't true. I get excited every single time I start a new book. To me, each collection of pages bound together, smelling of dust and paper, is a potential adventure. But lazy editing, sloppy character arcs that look more like character lines, and gimmicky, unrealistic plots leave me wanting to nurse my wounds with authors I already know won't disappoint me. It doesn't have to be this way. I believe that every reader wants to give new or less-known writers a chance, but if they do, you had better not disappoint them. That is why we are going to spend an entire chapter learning what frustrates readers, why they stop reading, and how you can get them to the last page without them wanting to hurl your own book at you. Without readers, your book is dead before it's even written. But how do we make sure that our book is ready to be seen by our target market? It's time to delve into book services and all of the ways they help our manuscript get ready to be unveiled to the readers.

Book Services and Why They're Vital

Even though we mentioned that both of us are book services professionals, the reason we recommend using book services has nothing to do with our professions (though we would love to work with you because we believe in making your manuscript the best it can possibly be). The reason we recommend utilizing book services is because not only will they make your manuscript better, but they will also make you a better writer. Working with industry professionals that understand all the techniques, nuances, and target audiences will help you level-up in a way that surpasses what pure education can offer.

It isn't just the education we need, but also help in implementation. In the last section I mentioned that the second step was to bring your piece of art before your peers in order to gather feedback. The important thing to note is that this group of peers must be better educated and experienced than yourself in order to make your work of art better. For example, when you share your goals with a developmental editor, they go through your entire manuscript with those goals at the back of their mind, whispering objections any time those goals aren't met. Wouldn't you want such a powerful ally on your side? There also comes a point in every round of edits where you stare at one sentence for several hours. The understanding of what you could do to fix or change it eludes you, and you leave a note to come back to it. You realize that at this point if you don't know what to do, it's probably time to ask for help. When you have an excellent copyeditor on your side, you can make a comment that you need help fixing it, and move on *without* staring at it for hours and save that time. Fresh and experienced eyes make a big difference.

After working with a well-educated book services expert, you will be even more excited to get to the next step (or you might want to go throw up or pee your pants—both are acceptable). After you have your first round of feedback, it's time to unleash your story upon the world where readers, hungry to slurp words, phrases, and plot lines into their brains like famished lips suck fat wheat noodles dripping in umami broth, wait to consume your newest venture into the literary world. But before you get to that, let's take a look at the mechanics behind every perfect read. And maybe get some lunch. Now I'm hungry.

CHAPTER 4

CHARACTER IS QUEEN (OR KING)

Though each individual aspect of the book creation process is important, the way you write your character can either make or break your story. Let's face it, we all have a favorite book (or maybe a list of favorite books). But what makes our favorite book *the one*? I guarantee you that one of the main reasons you love that book so much is because of who the protagonist is (the word protagonist literally means "first fighter" in Greek). A protagonist's likability is a strong tool in the hands of any author. Without that, we wouldn't be able to make you root for our protag all of the way through the book. But what makes a main character the *main* character? And how do we take this fictional person and make people feel things in relation to them?

Then there's the other person, the antagonist (meaning "opposite fighter" in Greek), the force against which our protagonist must prevail. But how do we write more than a two-dimensional baddie? If we really want to engage our target audience, we must delight them with a character they love to hate, but can also relate to. Does that sound like a difficult feat to accomplish? It is, but that doesn't mean there isn't a simple formula you can use to run your antagonist through. Plus, just like we have a great historical collection of relatable protagonists, we have an equally rich list of examples we can examine in the antagonist realm as well.

We will discuss the plot more in detail later, but besides the plot, the protagonist has an additional path that leads them through the story called a character arc. This magical plan will help your reader understand and relate to your protagonist. In the world of main characters and character plots, we also have other terms that describe what kind of arc the character is involved in: dynamic character arcs involve a lot of challenges that change the way the character acts and thinks while a flat arc means the character pretty much does the same thing the entire book and doesn't change at all. We will go over which of these types of arcs is more effective in attaining reader involvement and emotion as we work our way through this chapter.

The last thing I want to discuss here is how to use outside forces (AKA circumstances) to propel the protagonist into change, or further cement them into their current patterns. You have to make your character move, and you can't do that by having them stay in one place without any outside influences. Whether you use other characters/relationships, locations, job details, things that are as seemingly abstract as weather, or all of the above, your character's ride in life is what shows the reader who they are. Good or bad, qualities about your protagonist won't reveal themselves unless you use something called an info dump, and readers generally hate this because they feel bored. In a match where listing everything about your protag goes up against showing the readers things about your main character through interesting scenes containing valuable interactions, the latter will win every time.

Protags That Stick With You

Take a trip down memory lane with me. I want you to think back to the first time you fell in love with a character. Whether it was on TV, in a movie, or in a book, what was it about that character that caused you to form a connection with them? For me, one of the most important character connections I made was with Nyle, a teenage girl living on a sheep farm in Vermont that is going through the deadly aftermath of a nuclear power plant meltdown. In her middle grade book *Phoenix Rising*, Karen Hesse creates a world full of death and despair punctuated with notes of hope for a different future. But what was it about Nyle that created that emotional bond? Well, when I read it, I was a teenager just like Nyle. She also did everyday normal things like cook pancakes (shaped like sheep, but still), clean her house, flip french fries at friends in the local diner, run errands for her Gran, and fall in love. Along with Nyle's normalities, she also had intense struggles, which I could relate to on one level. No, no one in my family has ever died of radiation poisoning. However, I understood painful family relationships and wanting to feel loved.

When a character experiences realistic struggles and the emotions that go along with them, the reader is won over. But in order to understand how to write characters that live in such a way, the writer must first experience all of the emotions that normal life brings. This is one of the reasons why, as you get older, your writing gets better. You have more life experience. Younger people who have been through a lot generally have more to say, but that doesn't mean you have to have had some traumatic event in your life to be an effective writer. You can supplement life experience for reading good books about complex issues until you live through a few yourself. But what makes a likable character likable anyway? If we add realistic struggles to any character, can we guarantee that readers will find them lovable and relatable?

Think back to the character I asked you about earlier, the first character you really connected with. Was it simply because of their struggles that you discovered that first kindred spirit? The thing that intimidates people that are new to character creation is that these beings—though fictional—must be so complex. They have to have their own sets of morals, desires, boundaries, goals, and deal-breakers. But what if I told you that I can guarantee that you will have a love-worthy character if you follow a series of instructions for every character profile you make? Would you be interested? Good, because I want to help you write a winning protagonist every time. But before we can write a great main character, we have to shape who that character will be. Let's get started on character profile creation.

Creating Character Profiles

At some point in learning how to write, I had read a book that said you should make a profile for your main character, so I did. The problem was that I couldn't remember the physical characteristics, ticks, and traits of the other characters and spent a huge amount of time during my editing phase hunting down all of the green eyes that should be gray and so on. Learn from my mistake. Though your supporting characters don't each need to have an extensive character profile like your protagonist does, don't leave them out of this process completely. It is fun to plug in information about your 2D characters as you go, in case you need someone to be a plumber or to be related to a celebrity character, but when you decide something about any character, write it in their profile. But what *is* a character profile?

Every character profile should contain things that you might not remember to incorporate in each character otherwise. Think about how many times you might have to look through your manuscript to remember the color of the hair of your protag's love-interest if you don't have an easy-to-access character profile to pull up. If you use writing software like Scrivener, there are built-in options for creating character profiles with names, descriptions, and areas for backstory. There are even spots where you can insert an inspirational picture to use as a template for the way your character looks. But you can also create your own character profile in any word processing software using the following list.

Character Profile
Name:
Birthday/Age:
Physical description (gender, build, skin tone, eye color, hair color, scars, unique features):
Education level:
Occupation:
Main ambition in life:
Immediate family members (ages, occupations):
Things they're afraid of:
Emotional and physical strengths:
Emotional and physical weaknesses:
Physical ticks:

Endearing qualities:
Hobbies:
Ultimate story goal:
Potential obstacles:

If you create a list that addresses all of these issues, you will be able to refer to it as you write your story, and will thus keep your character consistent throughout. Even as your protags or supporting characters change within their arcs (we're going to discuss that in the next section) your character profile will serve as a map that shows you where to go next. If writing a character profile for a fictional person seems intimidating, why not try writing one for yourself? In fact, I'll use my own life as an example for your benefit.

Character Profile

Name: Kristin Noelle Spencer

Birthday/Age: December 20th, 36
Physical description (gender, build, skin tone, height, eye color, hair color and quality, scars, unique features): Female, plus-sized; fair skin; 5'6", blue eyes, thin and curly hair that has been dyed purple; scars on right knee, stomach, and over left eye; wears blue thick-framed tortoise glasses for astigmatisms and myopia; has large watercolor tattoo on left forearm and wedding ring tattoo on left ring finger; rarely wears makeup; always wears three rings; has three piercings in right ear and two in left. (Also, if I get murdered, here is a great description for people identifying my body)
Education level: BA in Comparative World Literature,

certificate of completion of Missions Training
program from Bible College, halfway through
Certification Program for Copyediting

Occupation: Writer, Developmental Editor, Copyeditor
In Training

Main ambition in life: To follow the teachings of
Jesus; to be a good wife and mom; to write full time;
to inspire others to follow their dreams

Immediate family members (ages, occupations):
Travis, husband, professional painter; Brian, dad,
licensed contractor; Peggy, mom, retired; Brandon,
younger brother, computer programmer (I'm going
to leave my family members' ages out along with
the names of my kids because... well, you know,
privacy and so forth).

Things they're afraid of: Talking on the phone,
meeting new people, large crowds, clowns, clones,
and robots.

Emotional and Physical Strengths: Supportive, not
judgmental, in general emotionally healthy, has
recently acquired arches in feet using barefoot shoes

Emotional and Physical Weaknesses: Boundary issues,
daddy issues, bulging disc in back, subluxing patella
in right knee (can't participate in sports, run, or
walk long distances), and tendinitis in hands due to
playing cymbals in drum and bugle corp plus typing
thousands of words every day.

Physical ticks: Always plays with hair, leaving copious
amounts of dandruff all over shirts and jackets;
pushes glasses up on nose a zillion times a day;
plays with rings in various ways, prefers to sit with

legs up on something due to knee pain and always tries to sit up straight to prevent more back pain.
Endearing qualities: Loyal, hard-working, always striving for the underdog or dark horse, loves to talk about stories of any kind (including real ones belonging to real people).
Hobbies: hanging out with family, sewing, paper crafting, reading books and comics, listening to music, thinking about things, redecorating old houses and buildings
Ultimate story goal: To never give up on her dreams.
Potential obstacles: Money; balancing being a mom, wife, writer, and editor; discouragement due to lack of acknowledgement by peers.

Wow, I just told you enough about myself that I could be a character in one of your books. But see, that's what a character profile does. Remember that all of this information probably won't make it into your book, but if you get stuck and wonder what your character would do in response to certain setting and plot driven stimuli, you can look back at the profile you created and base their actions on what you already know about them. And now that you know so much about your character, it's time to decide how to create and shape the thing that moves the story forward: the character arc.

The Character Arc de Triomphe

If you want to create a protagonist that people will root for, you need to do several things to make the necessary tension you must write into any story more bearable. Readers are willing to go on a ride with you as your protag races toward the finish line of your plot, but if you don't add in some moments of comfort along the way, a lot of readers won't want to go through the stress of reading any of your books again. But how can you accomplish everything at once? The short answer is, create a dynamic character arc.

Flawless people don't exist. It's a fact. Can you name any unerring person aside from Jesus Christ (even then I know a lot of people wouldn't include him on that list)? That's what I thought. This means that flawless characters shouldn't exist. Perfect protagonists are not just boring, they're unbearable. You have to decide right away what your protag's flaws will be, but you also need to decide which of these flaws will change throughout their journey. This is the way to win readers over, make some of the flaws things that the protagonist is willing to change after they go through some of the difficult circumstances that make up your plot. For example, if a male character is a womanizer, that's fine because it's realistic. But don't leave him that way. Your readers will never get on board with that long-term. The trick here is to make the change of heart costly to your character. If it happens without a second thought, how plausible is that? People who have held onto certain opinions for years are hard-pressed to change. But, I'm getting ahead of myself. What *is* a character arc?

A character arc is the process that happens as the protagonist changes over the course of your story due to changed circumstances. If a character is already happy and healthy, they probably won't have a dynamic (or powerful) character arc, because they have already done a lot of changing. In other words, if you give your protagonist a boring life without any exterior forces, you will probably have a dull book on your hands.

For those authors who are successfully able to engage readers with a linear character arc (AKA no character arc), well, we call them masters. Writers like Henry David Thoreau or Joseph Conrad come to mind. I'm not saying you *have* to have an arc for your protagonist. Maybe you want to write the sort of story where your protagonist has the same unbending belief through the entire book. In that case, you had better create an amazing cast of supporting characters that *have* dynamic arcs as a direct result of their interactions with the main character. There must be characters in every story without arcs. We can't have every character possess a complicated arc, it would be too much. Though it is more common these days to have as many as six points of view meaning that there are that many protags (I'm looking at you The Expanse Series), not all of the characters change or transform throughout the story.

It is a general rule that there must be a cast of supporting characters, just as there have to be subplots. In a similar way that subplots function in order to give the reader time to take a break from the main plot so that the book isn't over as quickly, supporting characters also provide readers an opportunity to take a break from the protagonist. However, the 2D characters (our supporting cast members), also offer a unique opportunity to provide the reader with secondary opinions and information about the protagonist that can either make us angry with the main character or love them even more. Think back to some of your favorite protagonists. Now, think about the people that existed around them. Were they likable? Did their opinions of the main character have something to do with influencing yours? In this chapter we are going to look at a notorious character, Dr. Gregory House, a narcissistic diagnostician who we tolerated for way too many years. I will argue here that the only reason we tolerated him at all was because the characters that surrounded him were uncharacteristically good-hearted. They rooted for House, and because of that, so did we. It turns out, that was a big mistake, and like all of the supporting characters (save one) we should have taken the hint and abandoned House as well.

If you want to endear the reader to your protagonist, surround them with likable supporting characters. They will win you a lot of favor, and if your protagonist is going to take just a little too long on their individual arc, this will buy you a ton of time. Now let's look at another kind of protagonist, one that many authors like to tackle for the seeming difficulty alone: the anti-hero.

So You Want To Write An Anti-Hero

Well, you're in luck. I want to prepare you for every type of writing success you can have, and the anti-hero seems like a good candidate if you want to journey the road less traveled. Before we get into it, I have to make a serious confession to you. I am something of a super hero junkie. Ever since I was a pre-teen, watching the cartoon version of X-Men every Saturday morning, I have been hooked. We even had to wake up early to watch it back then... I mean, I could have used a VCR to tape it, if we had had the programmable type, but we didn't. I have seen every single Marvel movie many, many times. My allegiance to Michael Keaton due to his portrayal of my favorite version of Batman is life-long. But for this example, I'm going branch into a different comic universe, because I myself am a Dark Horse. If you're as nerdy as I am, I hope that last sentence made your heart skip a beat, and if that's the case, you probably already know where I'm headed. Who is the ultimate example of a successful anti-hero? That's right, Hellboy. For the purposes of this lesson, I'm going to be basing my suppositions on the Guillermo Del Toro films from the early 2000s. That way you don't have to go out and buy several hundred dollars' worth of comics (like I did before Captain Marvel came out).

The main reason that Hellboy is perceived as an anti-hero is not that he's actually evil at all. It's his origin story coupled with his appearance that make the other characters around him naturally distrust him. If we look at all of the facts of his record, having been raised by a loving adoptive father whilst also being born as the literal spawn of Satan, it doesn't even seem fair that people treat him as a potentially dangerous villain, ready to embrace his evil past at any moment. It is *because* of the behavior of others that Hellboy is the cantankerous, though deep down good guy he is. But how do you get past all of his annoying habits? He pushes everyone he loves away, and he's mean to everyone he doesn't push away. Yes, he's strong and helpful, but he also makes huge mistakes based on his ego and pride that cost the people around him. So why do we continue to root for him? This is the question you must ask yourself before you start to write any anti-hero. If you can't answer it, you're doomed before you start, or should I say damned?

Every anti-hero must have at least (but probably more than) one redeemable quality that keeps the reader on their team. For Hellboy, it is that he has a huge ability to love, even though he seems to resist showing that ability to most. We know he loves his father, and he's in love with Liz. Think about Venom, another anti-hero. He's an alien that has come from another planet in search of consumable resources (AKA human beings), but when we see his choices and his relationship with Eddie Brock, we learn that Venom can change and adapt into something much more palatable to us as readers/viewers. Then the switch comes, at one point we had only been rooting for Brock, but then Venom becomes a relatable character. Does he still murder people so that he can stay alive? Yes, but we like him because now he only murders bad people, just like Jeff Lindsay's *Dexter*. You can also set up this sort of story for your own anti-hero. Give them a compelling backstory, good friends, and relatable and redeemable qualities to balance out their flaws and loose ethics and you've got a winner on your hands.

The Worst Kind of Anti-Hero

In the last section, I mentioned that we were going to talk about Dr. Gregory House as an anti-hero. Though he has no likable qualities aside from his one heroic aspect (more on that in a second), we root for him because of the supporting cast of characters around him. They all have compelling character arcs and because of that, we automatically root for House by proxy. If they see something good in him, it must be there, right? But the sad news is, it isn't. House doesn't really change, and any short-term changes we see are soon undone by his constant self-sabotaging nature.

The only truly heroic thing about him is that he uses his genius to help people live. But the *reason* he does it is also flawed. He thinks of it as a game. And for a while we can sort of tolerate that, but it gets old really fast. If you want to make your readers mad at you forever, create a character like House. However, if you want to win readers over while writing a compelling anti-hero, you have to give the protagonist redeemable qualities, or at least the possibility of future change for the better. I'll step off my soap box now. Let's get to the other guy. The antagonist.

An Antagonist You'll Love To Hate

To write a successful story, you must have forces for your protagonist to butt up against. That's how it works. Your forces could be as abstract as fate or the environment, but they must be there. And because of this, writers often choose a face and a name to represent that force, and so, we must now discuss that shrouded figure: the antagonist.

Imagine you were created as a slave race, but because you were created sentient, you realize how messed up that is and you decide to rebel. You're more technologically and physically gifted than your creator and you feel that your liberation is at hand. But instead of completely destroying your creators, you decide to disappear entirely because the whole situation is just so depressing. But no matter what you do or where you go, your creators just won't leave you alone. Fine, then, if they want war, you'll bring it, and you play to win. I have just described the complicated backstory of the group of antagonists from the legendary television show Battle Star Galactica (BSG). In the scenario you just read, you were a Cylon. What the frack, right?

When you first start watching the BSG reboot (created in the 2000s), you have no idea why the Cylons want to obliterate all of humanity. It doesn't make sense, or so it seems, because we don't know their villainous backstory yet. Once we find out everything, we understand what their motivation is, and we realize, "Wait, have I been rooting for the actual bad guys all along?" If only it were that simple. Though I was extremely displeased with the final episode from a storytelling standpoint (and no, you won't change my mind about it), this show is a great example of how a well-positioned backstory can endear the reader to your antagonist. But why would you ever want to do a thing like that? You want your reader rooting for the protagonist, don't you? Well, yes and no. Allow me to elaborate.

During the character-planning stages you have several popular options to choose from when you think about which type of antagonist you want to employ.

Later on, we're going to discuss empathy-based writing as opposed to preachy writing. Your antagonist can play a role in utilizing empathy-based writing in that having a complicated character as your antagonist can create moments of realization, relation, and change in your protagonist. However, you can also choose to create an antagonist who does nothing but create tension. These are the kind of baddies we love to hate. But even then, there is a formulaic approach that will relieve a tiny bit of tension in the reader, despite the antagonist's can-kill attitude: make the antagonist believe that what they are doing is actually the right thing to do. This self-deluded path will endear your antagonist to the reader, but not enough for your reader to want your baddie to overcome your protag. Because of this phenomenon, there are huge groups of people that love Disney villains, Moriarty, and countless other classic antagonists. Give us a bad gal or guy we love to hate, and you're well on your way to writing the perfect read. But what about stories that don't have one (or a group of) specific antagonists? What then?

Force Of Pen And Paper

Real life is full of unexpected and unpredictable twists and turns. Whether or not we have an actual antagonist in the story of our lives, there are outside circumstances that act upon us all the time. The result of this constant exterior influence is that we are forced to make choices constantly. If you want to have a baddie-free story, no problem, but you have to figure out what havoc your protagonist will endure and overcome (or survive) so that you can show either how they change according to their arc, or how they influence other characters to change via secondary character arcs.

Say it with me, "We torture them because we love

them." That's going to be our mantra as we talk about how important it is to create an environment of opportunities for change for our protagonists. If no exterior forces come into the lives of our main characters to give them opportunities to learn and grow, there is no reasonable way that they can change. That is a pretty big hurdle considering that we are supposed to watch their journey of transformation throughout the book. As artists, we take concepts from real life and apply them to our art. That is a huge part of the artistic process. Even if you are writing about the fae and their almost-immortal state of being, there must be hurdles for them to overcome unless you want to end up with a mundane story. But how do we wield these forces, and what are the forces we need to wield?

There is a plethora of options when it comes to employing outside forces. Maybe your protag and their rag-tag crew are up against insane weather while sailing on the ocean. It could be that your main character has an insane family that thwarts their every effort to become a healthy human being emotionally and physically. Maybe they have an illness that keeps them from pursuing their life goal and they decided to go for it anyway. These forces can be as little as a grumpy customer that causes a retail associate to get fired or a bad haircut. The most important thing to remember when choosing the exterior circumstances for your main character is that your job is to make the reader feel the way you want them to feel, for better or for worse, so your circumstances have to assist in that goal. If your character is feeling awful and you want your reader to feel awful, you have to make sure that the thing that happened to your character is bad enough that it evokes emotion in the reader. Like I said before, we torture them because we love them.

In her book *In The Unlikely Event* (a book this humble reader suggests every fellow-reader should read), Judy

Blume takes the protag, Miri, through some of the most heart-breaking circumstances any human being can experience. After four airplanes crash in her tiny town within a time span of just a few months, Miri's life changes in intense ways. I don't want to spoil the entire book for you, so I won't mention too many of the actions Blume uses to accomplish making the reader respond to Miri's plight, but I will share one example. Miri experiences the aftermath of one of the crashes when she runs to make sure her beau isn't killed after a plane smashes into a property near the house where her boyfriend lives. As readers, we experience Miri's emotional and physical trauma as a result of experiencing the sights, sounds, and smells of a large number of people dying and then being burned in the fiery flames that erupt as a result of the accident. Did I cry with Miri? You bet. Was I sorry that those things happened to a character I was so connected to? Of course. But that's the point. Blume is a master, and because of that, she made me feel the way she wanted me to feel. In this case, she wanted me to feel sorrow because that's what Miri felt. Exterior circumstances are some of the best tools you have at your disposal to make your reader feel the way you want them to. Don't forget about the forces you can create with pen and paper.

CHAPTER 5

SET IT UP

Whenever we think about the setting of the story, something simple often pops into our mind. We usually think of a geographic location, whether fictional or based on a real place. But what we don't realize is that the setting of our story is an extremely useful tool that can give us so much of the background information we need. If we would change the way we approach setting during the outlining stages of our writing preparation, we would be able to write more compelling stories in a shorter amount of time.

Another popular stigma that has to do with setting is that if you are writing within the fantasy or science fiction genre, you have to worldbuild, but for the other genres, you can easily skip over that process. Every part of your protag's experience in their world is a foregone conclusion unless you're writing about elves, fairies, wizards, or extra-terrestrial beings. Well, that couldn't be further from the truth. Even if you're writing something you think is exceptionally ordinary like contemporary fiction, you must know how your character interacts with the world around them. In fact, if you get something *wrong* in contemporary fiction, readers are way more likely to notice it. I can't tell you how many emails I've gotten about my fictional series set in Southern California (where I grew up), because I called the place a Junior High instead of a Middle School, a detail I had known, but chosen to change for naming reasons. In the relaunch, you can bet I'm going to correct all of those names in all three books in the series. But before I can tell you the *how* of setting, I need to expand on the typical definition of the *what.*

The Setting: Worldbuilding For Every Genre

It is this humble writer's opinion that the words "setting" and "worldbuilding" are completely interchangeable. I know that to synonymize these terms may make a lot of old-school teachers and professors uncomfortable, but it's not really the terms I want to emphasize anyway: it's the process. Let's take a look at the definitions of each word.

set·ting /ˈsediNG/ *noun*
the geographical location or physical surroundings where an object is positioned. a time in which some literary or visual work such as a play or novel is represented as taking place.

world build·ing /wərld/ /ˈbildiNG/ *noun*
a process where a writer creates an entire world where their protagonist(s) will exist and interact, sometimes within a well-planned universe. such

worlds are used to enrich the story by giving the protagonist(s) forces with which to interact.

See what I mean? Two different terms, two definitions that mean the same thing: synonyms. The issue that I have with both of these definitions is that neither of them really explains the importance or scope of setting/worldbuilding. For that reason, I want to show you a more detailed list of everything you ought to think about/plan when you are setting up your fictional world.

Setting/Worldbuilding Considerations
    -Geographical location on planet (world, country, state/dominion, county, city, village)
    -Topography
    -Weather patterns
    -Local, national, and worldwide political influence
    -Available technology
    -How they tell time
    -Language usage (slang and vocabulary changes over time)
    -Gender and race relations
    -Family structure and approaches to parenting
    -Cultural practices and attributes including their system of religion
    -Food
    -Music
    -Wildlife
    -Plant life
    -Relationship structures outside of family life

Though this list may seem intimidating at first, if you

write even a small sentence about each item, you will take far fewer fact-finding detours when you sit down to write your manuscript. This list should also change the way you think about your story because you can use environmental, political, religious, and family forces to propel your plot and protagonist forward. Think about this information as a list of possibilities, and your attitude about creating will shift from daunted to determined.

When Worldbuilding Becomes A Distraction

There is one major caveat I should share with you about worldbuilding: it can become addictive. You might think I'm joking, but ask any worldbuilding aficionado how easy it is to fall into the trap of relentless worldbuilding. The problem with getting too wrapped up in creating your world, its systems, and all of the possible characters that live there is that you will spend time working on things that will never go into your book, and you will waste time that could be spent writing thinking up this unsharable amount of information. Here is the argument I hear most often when I tell people to put their worldbuilding bible down and actually write: "But I'm going to write five books, or maybe even more, about this world. Isn't it reasonable to spend a year fleshing out all of the details?" No, it's really not. But why?

If you spend time writing, you will get better at writing. As a writer, that should be one of your biggest goals. Get words in every day. If not every day, at least three times a week. In contrast, when you spend your time worldbuilding, you do *not* get better at writing. In fact, the more you delay writing your story by *investing* time in your fictional world hashing out all of the nuances of your lands and political agendas, the more difficult it will be for you to start writing because sometimes as worldbuilding starts to feel comfortable, writing starts to feel scary. Don't let yourself get caught in that trap. Different books (or series) will need different scopes of background information, but once you know enough to start writing, write.

Don't Break Your Own Rules

There is a second trap that involves worldbuilding, which most readers find unforgivable. In the world of literature, we even have a name for this upsetting issue: deus ex machina, or in English, god from the machine. This happens when writers don't follow the rules they've established in their own setting, because they've written a problem that seems too difficult for their protagonist to solve. Let's look at the definition of this term.

Deus ex machina
A literary term that describes a plot device where a problem that seems impossible to solve in a story is cleared up all at once by something that is unforeseen, abrupt, and unlikely.

In general, unless you tip off your reader earlier in the plot that some supernatural being or idea has the potential to help your protagonist, deus ex machina reads like cheating to your readers. Think about your own experience as a reader. Have you read almost all the way through a novel, and then suddenly something happens that doesn't really seem to make sense, but it solves all of the problems of the protagonist? How did you feel when that happened?

The best way to avoid angering your readers in this

way is to follow your own rules. Whatever religion or magic-based elements you have in your setting need to remain to constant. You still get to decide what those elements are because you're the creator. However, you can't suddenly change the laws or magic or the way the religious beings work because you've written yourself into a tough spot. That is why we emphasize planning, because then you know what's coming ahead of time. But even the best planners sometimes get surprised by characters deciding to do things you never planned for them to do. That's okay. That's part of the fun of writing. Simply remind your characters that while it is fine for them to deviate from your plan from time to time, they must obey the laws of your universe.

Setting In Every Genre

Earlier, I touched on the idea that even when you write genres that don't seem to involve worldbuilding, you still have to consider the setting. While some genres scream "Worldbuild me," others may deceive you into thinking that you don't need to work through the setting while you are in the planning stages of your plot. The result is usually the oversimplification of setting, which will always insult your readers because it means that you were just plain lazy. When you don't put the work in, your readers will know. You are providing them with a service (entertainment) and when you get the details wrong, you are failing to deliver on an implied promise you've made to anyone who picks up your book. So how do you avoid setting errors that will create distrust between you and your readers?

Use the list mentioned in this chapter even if you feel like it's pointless. If you're writing about a book that's set in the town you grew up in, you still need to work through the points. When we visit or live in a place, it doesn't necessarily mean that we experience it as a writer, taking notes about music, culture, and wildlife. Filling out the list will help you think about the setting from a writing perspective. It is also good to give this setting sheet out to your critique group or editor because then they have an instant frame of reference, and can pick out any inconsistencies right away instead of having to leave their questions for a query (questions directed to you by the editor, not a query submission for an agent) or a second read-through. The list will force you to think about things you haven't thought about before. When I was writing *Plunge Into Darkness* I had decided that they had killed off all of the birds, but suddenly a bird sang in the distance. My writing group picked up on it right away and suggested I allow birds to be endangered instead of extinct. Maybe that seems like a small detail, but it doesn't matter how insignificant the information seems at the time if you end up weaving inconsistencies into your story. And because of that conversation you'd better believe there will be a scene about a bird in the final book (birds are full of potential for symbolism after all).

Using Setting For Contrast

Though the primary use of setting is to create a backdrop for the interactions of your protagonist, there are also creative ways to use your setting to highlight certain aspects of your story and characters. It is important to look at worldbuilding as a skilled tool. While most people might think of it as a hammer that connects two pieces of wood, in a pair of experienced hands, it can function more like a chisel to shape something complex and delicate like a wooden bird.

Two Settings, Two Choices

To illustrate the first particular function—using two settings to contrast character changes over the course of the story—I want to look at one of my favorite films, *Doc Hollywood*. This movie has a repeatable synopsis (so repeatable that the same actor is in a similarly-themed movie from 1993 called *For Love or Money*), but several elements hit home with me. It could be because I'm from Los Angeles, and I have seen the super superficial side, but I had no problem buying into the fact that Ben Stone (Michael J. Fox) would be a rich jerk as a result of working in the plastic surgery industry of Southern California in the 90s. Los Angeles is setting number one, and it paints a disparate picture of a life wasted pursuing financial wealth and fame. There is a much more beautiful side to my home town, but it is also vain and vapid, so good on you to all the screenwriters who have written it that way. The second setting is a small town in South Carolina. I have never lived in South Carolina, but I can say that having moved to a small town in Western Pennsylvania, and possessing a father from a small town in Missouri, small towns like the one depicted in the film that are community-centered do in fact exist. But why use two different settings?

In this film, Los Angeles and the fictional town of Grady, South Carolina both represent different life emphases that Stone must choose between. He can either have fame and money (Los Angeles), or he can have meaningful romantic love, community, and make a difference through medicine in a town that will lose its own doctor to retirement soon (Grady). I won't spoil the end for you, but I will tell you that if you want to see excellent acting and a great use of setting, you should watch *Doc Hollywood*. Did I mention that Woody Harrelson is in it? As far as I'm concerned, that gentleman can do no wrong. Do I have a Pop Vinyl figure of him? Hey, I'm a fangirl, alright? I thought you had already figured that out about me.

Setting and Multiple POVs

There is another practice that I'm sure you have noticed in other books and films, that setting can be an aid in indicating a change of point of view. This is particularly true in books that fall under fantasy, science fiction, or space fantasy genres, but it can be used in a number of other genres as well. If you like historical fiction, Rachel Hauck's writing serves as an excellent example of how to use time-related setting cues to emphasize changes in POV. Her characters often exist at the same geographical locations, but several decades apart. She uses details about technology, culture, and language usage (all different cogs in the worldbuilding machine) to help the reader adjust to the different time periods of each character.

You can also use contrasting geographical locations and cultures to help your reader delineate between changes in POV. You should always help your reader understand those changes with a simple clue at the beginning of a major transition in POV or time, but you can help them shift mentally into a different POV by utilizing multiple settings. One book series that is exemplary at this is *The Expanse* series by James S. A. Corey. These books have four to six separate POVs at any given time, and one of the things you can't wait for in each book is for the different POVs to intersect at one geographical location, whether that's on Mars, Io, or a spacecraft on the other side of the solar system. Because some of the characters are on different planets for a majority of each book, it makes it easy for the reader to follow along, shifting mind-frames as they switch POV. Remember that setting is a tool you can implement to emphasize things to readers in different ways. Don't underestimate all that worldbuilding can do for your story.

But what do you need in order to best utilize your setting? A good plot. And we're going to give you an industry-accepted full-proof plan that will work every time. But before we get to the next chapter where the plot thickens, let's take a slight pause at another station.

Narration Station

When I was thinking about where I should include a section on narration, I thought about where this issue naturally fits. It could easily go under both plot and character, as the style of narration affects both, but I thought, why not add it under setting, since the available information of the setting will definitely be affected by the type of narration? But what does narration mean, and what choices are available to you, the writer? And also, what is the difference between a narration and a narrative?

nar·ra·tion /nəˈrāSH(ə)n/ *noun*
the avenue which you employ to share your story with the reader.

nar·ra·tive /ˈnerədiv/
noun
a collection of corresponding events that, placed in line all together, create a story.
adjective
a form of writing employed in works such as essays and poems.

Think of the narrative as the story itself, while narration is the voice you utilize to tell it. Each narration choice is made up of two important decisions. First, you must decide the *who*. As far as the *who* of the narration is concerned, just think of third grade and personal pronouns. Here are the three possibilities of the different points of view (POV).

First Person: *I* saw that the tiny purple fiber on the stiff, dead body matched one that Janice had just plucked from her violet winter coat. (The author can choose which character the point of view is from, but it is often the protagonist.)

Second Person: *You* saw that the tiny purple fiber on the stiff, dead body matched one that Janice had just plucked from her violet winter coat.

Third Person: *She* saw that the tiny purple fiber on the stiff, dead body matched one that Janice had just plucked from her violet winter coat. (This choice also includes *He*, *They*, or an alternative pronoun such as *Xe*.)

Now that you know which *person* (or *POV*) you're writing in, you have to consider the scope of knowledge of the narrator: this is the second step.

Omniscient: The narrator knows everything and sees everything, giving the reader unrestricted access to what they need to know about the plot, setting, and characters.

Limited: In this case, the narrator of your story does not know all of the information involved with your characters, plot, and setting. This type of POV is usually used for first and second person narration.

Subjective: With one or more specific POVs, this

narration style utilizes the thoughts, feelings, and opinions of one to several characters.

Objective: An unbiased account of what happens in the narrative takes place here as the narrator does not include any particular point of view or feeling with this choice. It is often employed in journalistic works.

But how do you know which choices are the right fit for your story? This can be discovered by doing a writing exercise before or after you create your outline in various POVs employing different scopes of knowledge. Try writing any important scene from your story idea utilizing the different POVs and scopes over a few days. It's better to try each attempt on a different day so your writing is fresh. Then read through your scenes, and have a readerly friend read them as well. At this point, you should be able to tell which choices fit your story idea. Margaret Atwood—a famous author—has shared that part of her writing process sometimes involves extensive rewrites after she realizes that the POV she started with doesn't fit the way she wants it to. I personally prefer to get this part of the process over with before I get too much writing done on any given project. This is another example of how different writing processes work for different authors.

CHAPTER 6

PLOT IT OUT

If you have read many novels, it is likely that you have sensed that there is a pattern within each one that forms a familiar structure. Even though you can't exactly put your finger on what makes a story work, you *do* sense that specific stories work and others don't. In this chapter, I'm going to give you a basic outline most successful storytellers use, which I will break down into smaller parts. If you think you don't need an outline because you go with the flow and let the story unravel on its own, at least give me a chance to help you understand why planning is a valuable and vital tool. And don't worry, nobody is going to deprive you of the right to call yourself a *pantser*. I love *pantsers*. In fact, I used to be one. For the uninitiated writer, *pantsers*, otherwise known as organic writers, are those who write by the seat of their pants. At the other end of the spectrum, there are the outliners, more commonly called *planners*. Whichever group you identify with, you'll see that a little outlining can save you a lot of time, not because it will make you finish your first draft sooner (although this will be a positive side-effect), but because this first draft will be in a pretty good shape from the get-go. Additionally, having an outline will make things run more smoothly when you hit a rut.

But first, let's examine a quote that is often misattributed to Abraham Lincoln. "Give me six hours to chop down a tree and I will spend the first four sharpening the axe." Well, you can argue with me all you want, but who can argue with this mysterious woodsman? Do you think he was planning on procrastinating for the first four hours? Or was he aware that in order to be effective at a given task one needs to plan first?

This is one of the major reasons you need an outline. Some writers feel that outlines might prevent them from being productive or creative. Worry not. The outline is there to give you the necessary freedom in order to create your novel. As you'll see, there's plenty of room within this structure for you to develop your story and characters but also flaunt your amazing writing talent. Think of your outline as a glorified to-do list. You know you have to eventually get your two protagonists to meet and fall in love, but the *how* is completely up to you. Once you have the basic structure down, you can start adding the specifics with confidence, knowing that you have a solid foundation on which you will build your work. Plus, because of the way the outline is formed, it's easier to note down new ideas as they pop up in order to evaluate whether they fit in with the rest of your book.

The Beginning: Zero to Twenty-five Percent

This part, although not always action-packed, is crucial

to the entire book and it takes up almost one fourth of your novel's total length. Here, you take the time to set the tone of your novel, establish the type of narration, give information about the world the story is set in, introduce the protagonist or protagonists, and allow your reader to familiarize themselves with the story and the world. Spend some time showing your readers the protagonist's daily routine and give them a little backstory. Show—don't tell—what your protagonist's inner demons are. Have the readers learn what's at stake for the protagonist and make them empathize. They don't have to immediately like the protagonist. This might happen later or not at all. But when they empathize, you know they'll stick around to see what happens to the protagonist once the stakes have been raised. Combine this tantalizing treat of an opening with an inciting incident early on in the story, and you have yourself a hooked reader.

Another essential point in the beginning of every good novel is foreshadowing, a tiny or not-so-tiny hint of something major that happens later in the story. In order for the foreshadowing to work, this hint needs to be inconspicuous. Make sure that whatever this hint is, it is memorable enough for the reader to have an "aha" moment when the actual foreshadowed event finally takes place.

It is understandable that you can't wait to write about the big events that will kickstart your story's development, but remember that books are usually read in a linear fashion. Though there are books that flagrantly ignore linear restrictions (a perfect example of an author that does this is James Schannep with his Click Your Poison series). If you don't make the beginning strong enough with a little hook, few readers are going to invest more time on your story. Well begun is half done. Okay, in your case, a quarter done. It is also true that, with the increase in competition from fellow authors pumping out sometimes twenty-plus books a year, you need to establish what makes your story special right away. A cheat-code of sorts for accomplishing this is to use a flash-forward scene. Taunt the reader with one of your later plot points to ramp up the excitement, but don't let them see the outcome. Then flash back to the real beginning of your character's journey.

Plot Point #1

While the entirety of the first quarter is spent with the protagonist just being there, minding their own business, the last part of the beginning phase is where things shift. Say hello to Plot Point #1. This is the moment when we enter the second quarter of the story (at around twenty-five percent), in which we finally see the antagonistic force. It's the point when the protagonist realizes they need to face an opposing force, be it a person, creature or something else entirely. This is when we see our first big reaction from the protagonist. They are no longer oblivious to things, because something has happened that requires their attention and response. They now understand that a threat is upon them, but they have no way of knowing its size just yet. Don't have your protagonist attack anyone or anything at this point. It's way too early in the story. Have them try to assess the danger and work out a way to prepare to battle against it. That's what you and I would do, isn't it? Remember, your protagonist should remind us of a real person we can empathize with, not some larger-than-life superhero. And if you have done a good job in the previous phase, then this is where your reader starts rooting for your protagonist.

Pinch Point #1

Once you finish writing the first plot point, the hero is dealing with the fallout and you are working on getting to the second plot point. But in between these two, your pinch point comes into play. It occurs between the first two plot points (at around thirty-seven percent). This is to remind the reader of the existence of the antagonistic force and all the implications it may have on them. Show the readers what's at stake for your protag. Sometimes, the main character doesn't even need to know what the reader sees. You can give the reader insights into the things happening in the background that will be difficult for your character to thwart. The fact that the protagonist may be unaware of the size of the threat is what makes things even more dramatic and engaging.

Plot Point #2

Remember when I told you that the protagonist has no clear idea what they're up against in Plot Point #1? Well, the Midpoint changes that (and like its name implies, this happens around fifty percent). This is the moment in your story when the true stakes are unveiled. New information enters the plot and makes the protagonist understand the nature of what they are dealing with. The Midpoint is where your protagonist finds the motivation that empowers them to change states; they move from merely responding to the situation to engaging in full attack mode. They take their fate into their own hands and throw themselves into battle. This is where your protag's heroic qualities (or lack of these qualities) manifest themselves more clearly. It doesn't mean that the protagonist will emerge the battle victorious, though. It's not the time for that yet.

Pinch Point #2

Everything that has brought your protagonist to the point of making the decision to fight has not just happened at random. This is all part of the character arc. Your protagonist has grown and evolved. It's like when you play a video game and your hero levels up. They won't be able to fight the boss if they haven't first accumulated all those precious experience points. All this growth, however, doesn't take place in a vacuum. Things *around* your protagonist have also changed and evolved. The difficulty is growing bigger, too. So has the antagonist. Your second pinch point's mission is to show us exactly how much bigger. Remind the reader of what is at stake, but this time, add some venom. Your goal at this point is to use pacing to create a line of tension that pulls the reader's eyes through the rest of your pages. This pinch point takes place around sixty-three percent of the way through the story, between plot points two and three.

Plot Point #3

Good news! You're almost finished writing your novel! Not so good news for your protagonist, though. The end of the third quarter and beginning of the fourth one is when Plot Point #3 strikes. If you're going to include a plot twist, this is a great place to put it. Readers love and hate to be surprised at this point in the project. Just remember to use foreshadowing earlier if you are going to do something crazy in the final fourth of the book. Readers want to be surprised, but they don't want to be totally unprepared to ride this rollercoaster with you.

Like in Plot Point #1, this is when new information enters the story, but this should be the last time. Whatever new clue you've wanted to incorporate, this is your last chance to do it. Have you mentioned another character earlier? Here is when you show them to us. Have you foreshadowed something that hasn't happened yet? This is your last chance to get it in.

Plot Point #3 (which happens at around seventy-five percent) is when you play the rest of your cards and let your protagonist fight his or her last battle. By now, they should have been equipped with everything they need in order to confront the antagonistic force. Both the protagonist and the antagonist have learned each others' strengths and weaknesses. The reader has learned all there is to know about both of them, too and has had the chance to see what drives each character: to witness the substance of what has made them each who they are. If you have developed your story as you were supposed to by taking every aspect of the first triangle into consideration, you do not need any tricks in order to bring your story to a satisfying end.

The Conclusion: Resolution

The catalyst for the resolution should be your protagonist, not a *deus ex machina*. Though it is an effective plot device invented by the Ancient Greek dramatists, it is often frowned upon in modern times. You can't just have a random character appear out of nowhere and save the day. Everyone and everything we see from this moment must be based on information that has already been relayed to the reader. Remember all the experience points your protagonist has gathered throughout this journey? This is where all of that effort pays off. It is likely that their life points will all be expended during the final battle, but if they are, you have to make sure that their death isn't in vain.

The last part of your plot is one of the easiest and hardest to write. It's easy because it has probably been in your head ever since you began writing your story. It has had a long time to ferment by now. What began as a simple idea has since grown into a full-blown novel. The end is what you've been dying to write all along.

If it's a standalone novel, then make sure you have tied all loose ends before typing "THE END." You don't want confused readers closing the book wondering, "what did the gun in chapter 12 have to do with anything?" No matter how gripping a plot you've weaved, these questions will ultimately linger in readers' minds and they'll pop up at the end, demanding answers. Your job is to cover them all in a way that's conducive to the entire plot and character arc.

If this work is part of a trilogy (it could be a duology if you so desire, but trilogies are so hip), then you need to cover the questions concerning the basic theme of this book alone. You needn't try to resolve every issue raised in the story. The unresolved issues are the seeds you have planted now in preparation for your future works. Make them good though, because you will reap what you sow.

Subplots and Scene Structure

Subplots are as necessary for a novel as daily routines are for a writer. One of the reasons is that without them, your work would not qualify for a full-blown novel, but rather a short story since there is not enough time or length in a short story to write complete subplots. In a novel, however, you are given both the time and the tools needed in order to write one or more subplots, depending on the total length of your project and the surrounding characters. It is important to remember that your subplots must involve someone else besides your main protagonist. The point of your subplot may not be evident from the start and that's perfectly okay. The goal is to add to the dimension of the story with meaningful interludes with other likable characters while buying time for your protagonist to struggle through their challenges on their way to the conclusion.

An effective subplot should check the following points: it should move the main plot forward; it should let the reader see some of the characteristics of the protagonist through another character's perspective; it should keep the reader interested while you're buying time to give them the information they need in order to solve the main plot.

I'm sure you have read a ton of books with great subplots, but I am going to use a quick example from a movie, which was based on a book. In *Jurassic Park*, the main plot revolves around the main protagonist, Dr. Alan Grant. It's his permission that John Hammond needs in order to open the park to the public. It's his resistance to accept dinosaur cloning that provides opposition. It's his character arc you see developing throughout the movie. One proof of that is how he is so hostile to children at the beginning of the movie, practically terrifying a poor chap, and how at the end of the movie, he puts himself in danger in order to save Hammond's two grandchildren, Lex and Tim. But what makes him risk his life in the first place? You guessed it, subplot. The computer operator, Dennis Nedry— although seeming innocent and nonthreatening at first —is the one character whose thirst for money unleashes T-Rex upon the protagonists. If it weren't for Dennis, Alan would have never needed to save himself and the children from the attacks of the dinosaurs and become the catalyst for the resolution of the plot. If this were the case, the movie would transform from a fast-paced dinosaur thriller in a total snooze-fest.

Scene Structure

If you think of a person you know as a hero in a novel, anyone who would read about them would soon lose interest. The reason is that in real life, humans develop so slowly that any change is insignificant in the present time. Learning a foreign language takes quite a few years, but in the pages of a book, it could all be over in a single paragraph with the magic of correct tense use. Everyday tasks are repetitive and dull. That's why you shouldn't write about them in detail. Plus, you won't have enough space in your book to include every little thing. To print each page costs a physical expense, and therefore every word should be treated as precious. But there will be a day in the life of your character where showing how they go through their morning routine matters. Don't leave out the small details just because they're small, but remember to include only relevant information that propels the plot forward.

Let's take a look at Chekhov's law: if a gun is introduced in Act I, then it has to be fired in Act II. The same goes for your character. Each scene, each action they do or interaction they have, must be there for a specific reason. If they fight with their spouse, for example, you have until the end of the book to resolve the issue and, through this resolution, your character needs to show signs of growth. You get to pick how the conflict will be resolved, like with couples therapy or even murder. But you cannot leave the reader wondering or your protagonist will still be at square one.

For all the above reasons, you should know how to structure your scenes in order to develop your character arc in tandem with the plot. As we've already seen, the plot of the novel has a particular structure. The same is true for each individual scene. Think of each scene as a novel at a smaller scale. Learning to handle individual scenes will help you handle the novel as a whole. As with the beginning of the novel, you need to give some information about the *where*, *when* and *who with*. Is your protagonist at work, alone late in the evening or maybe at a French bistro with a good friend for early brunch? Then you need to consider the *why*. Is this state something your protagonist is usually in or is it a special occasion? Finally, the questions need answering are the *what* and the *how*. What does your protagonist do in the scene? Are they giving or taking advice? Have they encountered a particular difficulty? Remember, key scenes at particular points in your plot must raise the stakes. Are they facing a major problem at work or at home? How do they handle it? Most importantly, do they emerge having changed from the circumstances of the encounter? *How* have they grown? Have they learned something that will help or inhibit them in their quest? Has their view of the world changed? Has any relationship with the people around them changed for the better or for the worse? These are all factors you need to consider. Though this list may seem overwhelming, remember that this is exactly why you have your outline. A word to the wise: always think on paper.

Remember when we discussed the novel's conclusion? Well, you cannot end *every* scene with a resolution. Save that for the scenes where you'll start tying up loose ends. But also make sure to end every scene with a transitional sentence that creates a hook-like element in order to keep the reader moving faster and faster toward the end.

See for Yourself

After you are done with the outline, try this: for the next novel you read or movie you watch, take notice of whether the author or director has followed this basic structure. If you have an ebook, looking at the percentages might amaze you. Maybe they do not correspond exactly to the ones you have seen in the previous sections, but the basic elements will be there. Have fun!

Pace the Race

Every year in Bird in Hand, Pennsylvania, runners from all over the world come to a small Amish farming community to try for a new personal record. But why Bird in Hand? Well, this race is known in the global running community for the consistent pacers. These Amish farmers, running in their long pants with their beautiful beards waving in the wind, consistently come in within several seconds of their pace times. Pacers in marathons attempt to run the race within a set amount of time, and runners who are aiming for similar times know that if they are near that particular pacer, their chances for finishing the race at their goal time is closer than if they made this attempt on their own. Because pacing is so important, this tiny, rural area in Pennsylvania has become a well-known staple among the marathon community. It also doesn't hurt that the course is gorgeous, covered in rolling hills and farmland, and that they have a family dinner for all of the runners for free after the race. But don't let me distract you with the idea of a delicious home-cooked meal for several hundred people. We're talking about pacing. But why are we talking about running a marathon in a book that's about writing fiction?

Though pacing is an important part of writing to master, this skill isn't limited to the pace of the entire book—scenes must also each be paced according to the overall pacing of the plot. When you run a marathon, you plan out *when* you want to arrive at each major section of the race, and adjust your pace accordingly. There is an understanding involved that if you run part of the race too fast or too slow that you will not be able to achieve your desired pace. The same thing is true about writing. You need to know *when* you need to arrive at each plot point and pinch point in order to get your reader to the right part of the story at the right time. Let's define this term specifically for writing, shall we?

pac·ing /pāsiNG/ *gerund*
rate of movement as the story progresses through the scene or manuscript. can also be thought of as the rate of flow of information and/or action.

Pacing is important because the way you write should move your reader quickly through the different parts of each scene in conjunction with your overall story. Each scene needs to have a beginning, a middle (usually where the main action happens), and an end (a response to the action). Then you need to set your reader up to a transition into the next scene and/or chapter.

Transitional sentences and phrases play an important role in successful pacing. These words and phrases act like narrative tour guides that alert your readers to how ideas connect and when they change. If you employ these little helpers correctly, they will create a seamless experience for your reader. In fiction, transition sentences can also be used to amp up the tension and cause the reader to keep going into the next scene or chapter. Imagine I ended a paragraph with a sentence like, "How could Stephen keep his mother from getting evicted from her apartment?" If you care about Stephen, and by extension, his mother, then you are going to keep reading, because you want to see how he solves the problem. Remember to include transitions when you're writing: they are pacing magic.

<u>Pacing Your Manuscript</u>

For overall manuscript pacing, you will need to use trial and error to figure out what method works best for you. I have a specific approach I use that my friend Judith refers to as, "using math." After I have finished my outline and decided on a general word count goal based on my genre's expected word count, I divide that number by 3,000 to figure how many chapters I will have. Some chapters will be shorter and some will be longer, but I know that in general, 3,000 words is a good chapter length for me, personally.

At this point, I also divide the overall number of my desired word count by four. This way, I know about where each plot point should happen. Then I divide the overall word count by three to determine where in the manuscript the pinch points should happen. I then look at my different chapters, and figure out where each plot point and pinch point should be placed and write a note about that in each corresponding chapter. For example, if my manuscript is 30,000 words, I will end up with ten chapters. I know that the first plot point should happen twenty-five percent of the way through the book. That means it needs to happen around 7,500 words, which means it will happen half way through chapter two (7,500 divided by 3,000 equals 2.5). On my outline under chapter two, I will make a note that says, "Plot point #1 - halfway through, usually with a note of what the plot point is (because if not, I'm not ready to move past the outlining phase).

This is my overall pacing process, and in general it works well for me (I don't always hit the exact percentages we discussed earlier in this chapter, but they are always close enough). If this seems too complicated for you, figure out your own process, but don't leave pacing out when you do your planning. A poorly paced story is one that readers will either quit or resent.

CHAPTER 7

THE WRITER: AN ELUSIVE CREATURE

We talk to babies from the moment they are born until eventually, after a year or more, they begin to form full, coherent sentences. This is natural linguistic development. A child gets a lot of input through listening and, with the help of their gradually maturing cognitive functions, they are able to provide output through speaking. The same process is true for reading and writing. First, you need input from the two receptive skills (listening and reading) and then you produce language through the two productive skills (speaking and writing). Makes sense, right? What I'm about to say here goes without saying, yet I constantly hear about aspiring writers who choose to disregard this popular advice.

If you want to write, you first have to read. A lot. Don't get me wrong, I don't mean only read books of the same genre as the one you're writing in, I mean read anything *good* you can get your hands on. By reading different types of writing not only will you build vocabulary, but you will also see how stories develop; you can discern the plot points and the pinch points we discussed in chapter 6; you can see other writing styles and even errors other authors make. That's why, apart from reading a lot, you should try to read types of writing you wouldn't otherwise read. Some examples are magazine articles, blog entries, nonfiction books, cookbooks, biographies, and memoirs. The reason why a reading variety is absolutely necessary is because it enriches your view of the world. It is true that the older a writer gets, the better they become. This happens not only because of the years of practice, but also the experiences they have accumulated. For a younger and/or inexperienced writer, reading like there's no tomorrow is a quicker way to bridge that gap.

The 20-Second Rule

Whenever we contemplate performing a task, we first have to start the engine from action to inaction, which basically means we need to change our current state. This involves decision-making and a certain amount of willpower in order to merely *begin* the task. As you have probably realized, once we start performing a task or activity, we usually have no problem sticking with it, like going to the gym. The problem is *before* getting there. How many times have you woken up, thinking you should go to the gym, but instead found excuses not to do so? Trust me, it's not just you. It may not seem so, but it takes a lot of mental energy to convince yourself to do something that you're not so crazy about doing. That's also why it's sometimes easier to work out in the morning instead of after work. Have you ever heard of "decision fatigue"? Sadly, our decision-making prowess begins to dwindle as the day progresses, which in turn can cloud our judgment and make us opt for the easier option instead of the more beneficial one.

The 20-second rule could help pave "the path of least resistance" as long as you know what to do. Let's say you want to write, but there are temptations in your environment that steer you away from your goal. After a long day at work, you get home, sit at the couch, and the TV remote is right there on the coffee table. The path of least resistance is to just pick it up and turn the TV on. It takes a second to do that. Your brain will gladly accommodate you, because it won't have to make any decisions. But, what if the remote was in another room, or hidden in a drawer somewhere in the house? What if it took you twenty or more seconds to get it? Your brain would immediately look for another, less energy-consuming alternative. Now, imagine that your laptop was on the coffee table instead, in sleep mode, with your writing program all fired up and waiting for just a tiny nudge to wake up. What is the path of least resistance?

I wish I could say we all had the ability to conquer our tendency to procrastinate, but some of us don't. That's why we need to trick our brains. For something that defines who is and who isn't a smart person, the brain itself is rather stupid. We need to decide what we need to accomplish and configure our environment in such a way so that it's easy for our brains to work with and for us. If you think it's impossible to kick the habit of watching TV after work, let me remind you that you weren't born with that habit. It developed through constant repetition, and now sitting at the couch is associated with watching TV. If you start to disassociate the couch with the TV and change the neuro-pathway connection, your brain will associate the couch to writing instead. It's not rocket science. Just plain old neuroscience. Always keep in mind that "cells that wire together, fire together."[1] Use this to your advantage.

Daily Routines

In this section, I'm going to give you some ideas you could use in order to start building your own daily writing routine. It's okay if you don't like all of them or you try them out and decide they're not for you; the same thing that can work for someone might not work for someone else. Boiling water can make an egg hard but a potato soft. In the end, they're both delicious.

When I first began writing more seriously, I tried to convince myself to view writing as a task; not a recreational activity. This meant that I had to prioritize it at the expense of other tasks and keep at it, even when I didn't feel like it. For a full-time writer, this is automatic behavior, but for non-professionals it could be a bit trickier.

In his book *Daily Rituals*, Mason Currey has cataloged the daily rituals of several artists and intellectuals. Some of them go to extremes, such as the Japanese author Haruki Murakami who wakes up at 04:00 and goes to bed at 21:00. Murakami justifies this strict regime by saying that it's his duty as a novelist to provide his readers, with whom he has an indispensable relationship, with books that show an improvement over his previous works. You might think that this personal sacrifice could even be compared to self-inflicted torture, but the point you are missing is that

---

[1] This is noted as a paraphrase from Donald O. Hebb's book *The Organization of Behavior*. The original attribution of this paraphrase could not be found.

this particular author has incorporated it into his daily routine. *Routine* is the operative word here. His waking up so early is routine because he does it without expending a ton of mental effort. Once you have your routine down, it's easier to stick to it and spend your precious energy on more demanding tasks. He also has vast reserves of self-discipline. He knows he wants to go running or swimming in the afternoon, so he has to be finished with his writing five or six hours after waking up. This means that Murakami is through with his most demanding task at roughly the time some people would like to wake up.

Now, don't think that this waking up before the sun is up as something that you must do in order to develop a daily writing habit. First you need to figure out your biological prime time (BPT). Murakami's BPT is obviously early in the morning. He's a lark type, since larks thrive in the early morning light. You might be the owl type and your creative juices flow better late at night. Or you might be something in between. The reason you need to know when you can perform better is simple. It will take you significantly less time and effort to write more and better when you do it during your BPT. You have probably heard of the 80/20 Rule, or the Pareto principle. This principle states that you accomplish 80% of your overall work in 20% of the time you dedicate to it. This automatically means that you pretty much waste 80% of time to only produce 20% of work. When you are sleepy, tired or your brain isn't yet fired up, you tend to waste more time than you can afford. But if you know exactly when you are at your peak performance, you can streamline the writing process, get more work done and get a feeling of accomplishment that will fuel the rest of your work of the day. And you will still have time left for other tasks.

In order to find your BPT, you must follow the "trial and error" approach. First, you have to experiment writing in different time slots throughout the day. Try to have stretches of uninterrupted time, say thirty to sixty minutes per session. Remember, your brain cannot start working at full speed the moment you sit down at your laptop. It takes a little warming up. But then, the remaining time in conjunction with the lack of distractions will work wonders for your writing. What you put on that proverbial paper will be more coherent. I personally use a variation of the Pomodoro technique, which you can tailor to your own needs as well. This technique is named after kitchen-timer that is shaped like a tomato (*pomodoro* in Italian). The basic technique is to set a timer (it doesn't really need to be tomato-shaped, don't worry) for twenty-five minutes. During that time, only write. Don't give in to distractions. It will help if you have silenced your phone or disabled the notifications.

One of my weaknesses is to stop working in order to look up something on the Internet, usually non-work-related. In order to battle this, I keep a small notepad nearby to jot down a memo to myself of all the things I "just have to" look up, do or ask after I have completed my day's work. You can find anything in there, from "Check out prices for a new food processor" to "Can you teach an ostrich how to speak?" (Spoiler alert: you can't.) Once the time is up, you can take a five-minute break. Use this for a bathroom break or to get a snack. Don't check Facebook, Twitter, Instagram and the like. The five minutes can easily turn to thirty if you get sucked in. Then, set the timer for another twenty-five minutes and repeat the process. After doing this for a period of twenty to thirty days, trying out different times and tracking your writing progress, you will most likely have discovered your BPT. And despite the fact that it takes some time to resume an interrupted task, your brain will be likely more prone to get back to work, because you will have conditioned it to do so; the time in-between writing sessions is not long enough for it to forget the task. But, again, don't expect to magically fine-tune your routine just after a month or two of writing. As most things in life, writing takes practice as well.

Practice

There's a famous quote, often attributed to either Somerset Maugham or William Faulkner, which encapsulates the importance that practice has for an author: "I only write when inspiration strikes. Fortunately, it strikes every morning at 9 o'clock sharp." If you are one of those people who daydream of some day having enough time or drive to write a book, this quote aims to burst your bubble. Writing is a profession. If you want to use writing to make a living, you need to show up every day. Writing is a craft. The more you practice and hone your skills, the better your end results will be.

I am now going to use a story from David Bayles' book *Art & Fear* as an example of why you need to keep writing even though you might think your work sucks. A pottery teacher once divided his students into two groups. He then announced to his students that he would give members of the first group, the *quantity* group, an A for producing fifty pots, a B for forty and so on. To the second group, however, the *quality* group, he said that each student only needed to produce a single pot, which would be graded according to its perfection. This meant that only perfect pots would be given an A. The findings of the experiment were astonishing. It turned out that the best-looking pots were produced not by the *quality* group, but by the *quantity* group. While all the students of the *quality* group theorized on the aspects that would make a pot perfect, the students of the *quantity* group kept making pots. It was through that repetition that they managed to hone their skills and produce great results.

The quote about inspiration two paragraphs earlier, no matter how thought-provoking, still fails to address the burning question: *how do I even begin to build a habit of writing daily so I can practice my craft?* James Clear gives a lot of pointers in his book, *Atomic Habits*, explaining how just a one percent of progress every day can compound throughout an entire year and yield amazing results. In his book, *The Compound Effect*, Darren Hardy also highlights the plausibility of massive results through small daily actions. In his book, *The 12 Week Year*, Brian P. Moran constantly stresses the significance of having a vision. To paraphrase Zig Ziglar, you cannot hit a target you can't see. If you combine these bits of expert advice, you will be able to envision what you want to accomplish and then start working on it every day, bit by bit. In his MasterClass, Dan Brown talks about something crazy awesome and effective that he did. He printed out a made-up cover for the book he was writing and stuck it onto another book, making it look like his book was already out in the world in physical form. By looking at it daily, he was able to keep himself motivated by believing it was within his grasp. This helped him finish writing it. You could do something similar in order to psych yourself up, too. The key is to do whatever you do consistently. You can dream all you want about the final straw that will break the camel's back, but your job is to make sure you load the poor animal with all of the previous straws, day after day.

Personally, I am an advocate of daily writing sessions. This is probably because I tend to detach from my material after a few days have passed, and the extra time it will take me to get reacquainted with a project I was already familiar with is time wasted. However, you don't have to follow the same path as mine if it seems too intimidating. You can easily set aside some time three days a week to focus your mental energy on your writing. This will be even more effective once you have found your BPT. And you never know, you might get into a groove and start adding more sessions throughout the week.

Writing Communities and Challenges

Something else you can do in order to keep your writing habit fresh and appealing is to challenge yourself. Everyone can take up running in the spring or summer when the weather is nice, but how do runners keep returning to the track when it's zero degrees out? They sign up for running events. They set goals and never lose focus of their target. So why not challenge yourself as well? The Instagram community has a lot of writing aficionados who create 30-day writing challenges every so often both for their followers, but also for themselves. Every November, there's also a worldwide writing challenge of writing 50,000 words in thirty days. At first sight, it seems overwhelming, but in reality you only need to write 1,667 words per day. See? That's the magic of the compound effect. Plus, through all of these events and challenges, you will have the opportunity to connect with fellow writers who will both teach you and learn from you.

Despite the fact that writing is considered a lonely sport, it's your fellow writers who will help you grow and improve. You can, of course, reach a certain level on your own, too, if you read books on writing and story structuring, but when you share the burden, you will get further than you had originally expected. The reason is because each of these individuals will bring to the table a certain quality you do not possess. Learning from different people makes your overall experience richer. You will have the chance to learn about their daily routines if they have any (if they don't, tell them to read this book), their approach to writing—whether they're *planners* or *pantsers*, whether they do extensive worldbuilding or they think that's only for fantasy writers (it's not). If your writing group includes some indie authors as well, you can find out all the steps you need to take in case you do not decide to take the traditional publishing route. It is also important to remember that the only way to know whether what you've written will resonate with a reader is to show your writing to one. Writers are also readers.

In his book *The Happiness Advantage*, Shawn Achor describes a terrifying experience he once had when he was a volunteer firefighter. After completing his basic training, he had to pass a final test, aptly called the "fire maze." The instructions given to him and his partner were simple. They had to enter a burning farm silo in order to rescue a dummy. Due to decreased visibility, his partner would be touching the wall in order not to get lost and Achor himself would be holding his partner's hand while sweeping the air with his free one. However, once the alarm on their oxygen tank went off, they both panicked and did the exact opposite of what they were supposed to do. If this had been a real-life scenario, they would both be dead along with the helpless dummy. This phenomenon is also common in workplaces, especially after a major— usually financial—disaster strikes. The employees tend to isolate themselves and ponder the losses the business suffered instead of teaming up in order to do some damage control and figure out their next steps. Why am I telling you all this? From personal experience, I have often caught myself doubting my abilities and playing that old record of crippling helplessness and utter defeat. During those times, one of my automatic responses is to just drop whatever I've been trying to do —in our case, writing—and focus on something that's less intimidating, but also considerably less rewarding. Only when I turned to my writing group for support did I manage to pick myself up and continue. I call this *shared pain*. When something unpleasant happens, I tend to blame my luck or my shortcomings as a default. But when I realize that the people in my group have also been through the same hell and have yet managed to persevere, I start getting my hopes up that I can do it too. Besides, one unshakable proof that something can be done is seeing that someone else has already done it.

<u>Why You Need All of This</u>
You may be thinking that all the above advice isn't for you before you try to employ any of it. But the reason why I think you should start building your environment around your writing routine right now is because I want to see your novel in a bookstore some day. If you don't create the conditions that will enable you to pursue your passion in the most productive way possible, that day may never come. While you may have managed to sustain a streak of productivity for a few weeks, the dreaded rut awaits you. If you are not confident enough in your methods, the rut might be your undoing.

So, how do you get out of a rut? One thing I've learned after years of relentless experimentation and constant tweaking of my routines, is that once you have your systems up and running, the hard part is over. Maintenance, albeit daily, is really simple. Plus, the mere pleasure you get when you accomplish your tasks in the allotted time builds momentum that carries to the end of the day and leaves you feeling proud of yourself, thus setting you up for yet another productive day. But the moment you hit a rut is when the preparation you've done will really pay off. It's at times like these when a good system makes you get back on your feet and resume working in no time.

Some might sustain that good professionals never hit a rut. They never get dragged into meaningless, energy-sucking meanderings while they work on a project. If you are as lucky as them, then you can just skip to the next chapter. For the rest of you who realize there is a possibility that you could miss a few days of productive work, the next few paragraphs might be useful.

Think of a rut like a cold. If you get it, there's no way to un-get it. You have it. The question you need to ask is "How do I get over this fast?" Well, the thing is that all *you* have to do is rest and drink a lot of fluids. Your body, your *system*, will take care of the rest. In the rut analogy, it's your productivity that's ailing. You are in control of the systems that have been keeping it healthy all this time. So, what you need to do is acknowledge the situation, admit that you are indeed in a rut and ease yourself back into your routine. You can start by doing simple tasks, like turning on the laptop and reading some of your previous work. Look through your outline. Do some research. Remind yourself why you began this project. Bring to mind what drove you to pursue a writing career. Remember any good feedback you received on your writing from a writing group member or friend. Think of all those moments that you felt proud of yourself over a small win while writing. What you shouldn't do, though, is expect your productivity to kick in immediately after that. Don't forget, healing takes time. If you try to force yourself to work while riddled with self-doubt, the outcome will most likely be sub-par. Plus, it might make a bigger dent to your confidence too, which might result in your rut period getting longer. When you keep working while sick, your cold takes longer to go away, doesn't it?

You Are What You Is

Even though we associate the above title to a famous song that urges the listener to embrace their own culture and be themselves, the sad truth is that it is grammatically incorrect. The error does not prevent us from understanding the meaning, of course, but if we had to read a text that was riddled with similar errors, we would get a headache—or an eye-ache. As a teacher, I've had my share of such texts, yet I know that my students are trying to learn a new language and experiment with its several nuances. What I always advise them to do in order to improve their grammar and spelling is to read a lot. I tell them that because I know that books have been through several checks that can guarantee that mistakes of such caliber have been corrected. This way, my students can actually see the proper use of grammar and apply it to their own work. I myself learned more about proper spelling and grammar through book reading than schoolwork. Life is the best teacher, after all.

But what if you couldn't trust books? What if both the writer and the editor lacked basic knowledge of grammar use? That would be sad and quite dangerous. This is why in order to become a good writer, you first must invest considerable time in learning basic grammatical rules. Some people might argue that they do not really need to waste time learning grammar since there are editors who are paid to fix their mistakes. Time to employ yet another example. Let's say that you have a car which you keep well-maintained. You check the oil regularly, you make sure there's coolant in the radiator, you check the tire pressure, etc. When it's time to have it serviced, chances are the mechanic will only need to do basic maintenance tasks. This means that they will work less time on your car and you will pay less money than if the car was in a really bad state to begin with. In the second case, you would get your car back later and pay way more than if you had done a better job with its maintenance. Your manuscript is like that car. The more you take care of it, the sooner it will be ready for publication. And hiring an editor will not pierce a hole through your pocket. Also, some editors might not even agree to take your manuscript on in the first place if it's what they would consider a mess. Don't forget that confused readers stop reading; your editor is a reader too. Don't make it hard on them.

So, what should you do? I suggest that you pick up a quick grammar guide or a book like *The Elements of Style* by William Strunk Jr. It's compact and contains most of the things you need to know in order to present your editor with a well-combed manuscript. The only reason your text should contain errors is if you meant for them to be there. In such cases, these errors are encountered in instances when your character speaks or writes something. In the rare case the grammatical errors drive the plot forward, then this is something you need to discuss with your editor beforehand, so they won't begin making changes to things that shouldn't be changed.

Another simple, yet life-changing idea, is to just look it up. We live in the golden age of information which we can get promptly and, quite often, at no cost. What you would have otherwise spent several minutes looking up in a dictionary, grammar book, or encyclopedia, is now accessible by hitting a few keys on your keyboard. You can search online for help with spelling certain words, or clarification on the use of a preposition or a verb tense. Even if you are almost certain that what you're writing is correct both in grammar and spelling, it never hurts to double-check. Don't forget that there are some discrepancies between American and British English. You may be the former, for example, but one of your characters might be the latter. Wouldn't it seem odd if they spoke or wrote in the same way an American did?

If what I've told you just now seems like a hassle, think about your continued education in grammar and writing as part of your daily writing routine, and it won't seem like an extra step. What if you spent just fifteen minutes a day on learning something new about your craft? Would that seem like such a great expense of time and effort? Probably not, and I guarantee you that the compound effect it would have on your writing over time would be totally worth every second and penny spent.

How To Win At Writing

The secret to win at writing is quite simple. If you only do one thing in your book, do this: make the reader feel the feelings you want them to feel, good or bad. Don't try to impress them or force them to like your book. If you have written with the reader in mind, that will translate into credibility with the reader. Respect the time they have dedicated to reading your creation. They could have chosen another among thousands of others.

Since your sole concern is the reader, it is important to understand that readers respond positively to empathy-driven projects as opposed to ones that preach at them. In his first published novel, *Carrie*, Stephen King introduces the eponymous character on the day she gets her period for the first time, at age sixteen. It happens in the school showers, while all of her girl classmates are present. Having been raised by an authoritarian and zealot mother with no parenting skills whatsoever, Carrie has no idea what is happening to her. As a result, she panics, thinking she is going to bleed to death. Amused at her confusion, some classmates start throwing tampons at her, chanting "plug it up." After only a moment's hesitation, another one chimes in, telling herself "There's no harm in it really." This scene is only a few pages long, but it resonates through the entire story. There are bullies and there is the victim. The reader has the chance to experience both sides. Stephen King never needs to *explain* why he thinks bullying is immoral. The reader can feel it.

The Curse Of The Second Novel

In 2014, I read a book that made all other books seem lame in comparison. It was Ernest Cline's *Ready Player One*. I've been suggesting this book to people for years. I used to say, "Oh, you just *have* to read this book." Now I still say the same thing, only I add a bit at the end. "Just don't read his second novel. You'll hate it." You know how I know they won't like the second book? Because I read it and didn't like it. Why did I read it in the first place, you ask? Because I thought I would get hooked on it like I did on his first one. I trusted the author because of how masterful he was at writing his first novel. I was willing to go on another thrilling ride with him. Boy, was I wrong.

Other authors have also fallen victim to trying to reproduce the success of their first novel by trying to write the exact same type of book with slight variations and tweaks. Sadly, you can't catch a lightning in a bottle twice. If you look up this phrase in the dictionary, you will see it described as something *fleeting* and *ephemeral* which means it happens once and doesn't last long. Unfortunately, many publishers—when seeing what a hit a book becomes—force the author to deliver a second book in order to take advantage of the momentum. The author usually succumbs to the pressure and writes a book that's subpar.

One way to avoid this dreaded situation, is to write an entirely different book. As we saw earlier, there are certain steps you can take in order to construct an outline for your novel. The fact that you might have written a book that was a hit doesn't oblige you to try and write something similar. Your readers have already read the first book. What they want is not to reread it with different characters; they just want your voice again. That's what brought them back. Honor their loyalty and give them a new story. They deserve it.

Writing For Improved Reading Comprehension

Let's make one thing clear: all people who know how to read are readers. The fact that some *choose* not to read is a different story. You've probably heard this quote by Mark Twain: "A person who does not read has no advantage over the one who can't." The meaning of this saying is clear, but I would like to dig a little deeper instead of shaming the people who choose not to read. Undeniably, reading is a skill. This means it must be practiced in order for the user to enjoy its benefits. When we view it as a skill that can be learned, it is safe to start talking about experienced and inexperienced readers. When you write a book, you have no way of knowing who is going to read it. Your job is to improve all readers' reading comprehension, regardless of their experience level.

I'm not suggesting that you write in plain language, though. Your writing should be what you meant for it to be, but at the same time, you should use certain tools that will make it enjoyable for the inexperienced reader, while not making it boring to the experienced one.

There are many novels which do not follow the storyline from point A to point B. Sometimes there are time-jumps. There is a recent trend that advises authors to avoid labeling time-jumps or switches in point of view (POV) in order not to insult the readers' intelligence. This is not wise for two main reasons. If you write a book with unlabeled time-jumps, two things will most definitely happen: on the one hand, your experienced readers will get mad at you for making them work to be able to understand what is happening in *your* book and on the other, inexperienced readers will find the book too intimidating and will stop reading it altogether. Leaving out the POV is another huge mistake because it will take readers too long to figure out who is speaking or thinking. If you are going to use multiple POVs, we advise you to always, always label them. Remember, make your book as easy to read as possible. This has nothing to do with language use, but reader ease. If you leave it up to your reader to figure out things you already know and hold them hostages as far as dates and POV, you are going to end up with a frustrated customer. Remember that readers are customers, they have paid for a service, for the right to be entertained or enlightened by your writing. Don't torture them: they will never come back.

Elevated Writing VS. Literary Fiction

There is a debate on the topic of "serious literature" versus "regular writing." If you're anything like me, I'm sure you cringed when you read the heading. There are a lot of people who only label "literature" the works which are written in an elevated style. This means the prose is written with impeccable grammar and syntax and it is more often than not, distant from ordinary language usage. If you have read a classic work of fiction or watched a period drama, you will know what's considered elevated style. Modern novels are written in everyday language and, hence, cannot compare to classic works or be labeled "literature." Despite there being several contemporary authors who try to employ elevated writing, the result can oftentimes seem fake, like a caricature of the original thing. Let's look at the following definitions.

lit·er·a·ture /ˈlɪt(ə)rətʃə/ *noun*
written works, especially those considered of superior or lasting artistic merit.

fic·tion /ˈfɪkʃ(ə)n/ *noun*
literature in the form of prose, especially novels, that describes imaginary events and people.

While it is indeed true that what some people consider literature is defined by elevated writing, the fact that fiction is a *part of* literature does not change. Literature is written expression of feelings and thoughts by an individual towards other individuals he or she has not ever met or that were not even born at the time of writing. Literature can take one of the following three forms: fiction (prose), poetry, or drama. Each of these forms can in turn be subdivided to more sub-categories. For example, fiction is an umbrella term for a plethora of literary genres; science fiction, fantasy, horror, romance, cyber-punk, historical, etc. None of these genres is superior to the rest nor inferior. They all fall under the even bigger umbrella term *literature.*

Personally, I am not one of those people who only read "the classics." I have read some classic works, but the truth is I struggled quite a bit with the language. The fact that those works are canon does not prohibit any modern authors from allowing themselves to write naturally. Times have changed, and so has literature. Honestly, I'm glad it has.

Some might snub certain literary genres as mediocre or not literary at all. The truth is we need *all* types of genres. The world we live in is filled with billions of different people. That's why it can never be boring. Why not have a similar—albeit smaller-scale—variety of genres? People have different tastes in food, clothes, and love interests. They are entitled to like different types of books too. Reading the same type of book will not help readers broaden their horizons and see other points of view. However, the beauty of literature does not stop there. There's no legitimate reader who will only like a single genre. This is an area in which people can be "unfaithful" with no consequences.

CHAPTER 8

THE READER: YOUR MAIN SQUEEZE

Without readers, there would be no reason to write. Even authors that only write for themselves are readers. In one case, there was a book I wanted to write just for myself. It's still unpublished. But the way I interact with it now that it's written and edited is solely as a reader. I want to experience the struggles of the characters, the vivid setting, the romance, the grief, the tension. My desire to go along on a ride with these characters propels me to the last page. And there, I feel a release. The story is over. A rush of emotions flood my mind and it lasts for the next few days, weeks, or months.

Before you can understand what causes this response within the mind of a reader, you first must understand the reader's mind.

A Reader's Brain

We live in an amazing age. Scientists can study so many things, and interestingly, one of the things that seems to intrigue them is the way that reading affects the brain. In a study[2] done by Emory University in 2013, they looked at the way that reading changes the connections in the brain. Though the study was by no means conclusive, the results they found suggest a physical connection between a character in a book and the way our brain interprets reading about them. In this study, students were monitored every morning via MRI after reading for nine nights in a row and the connections between the parts of the brain that controlled physical stimulation and function contained in the left temporal cortex were improved. While interpreting the data, neuroscientist Professor Gregory S. Berns suggested that their findings have to do with physical sensation and movement systems within the brain and that this data may even imply that the action of reading a fictional book can take your brain into the physical body of the main character of the story. Berns also noted that these changes lasted up to five days after the participant of the study had finished reading. When you write an engaging story, you are physically changing the mind of your reader.

In fact, in another study[3] done by the Pew Research Center in 2012, readers explained that one of the main benefits of reading is that they are able to learn about the experiences of others in a way that allows them to be more open to looking at real-life situations from a

[2] https://www.psychologytoday.com/us/blog/the-athletes-way/201401/reading-fiction-improves-brain-connectivity-and-function
[3] https://www.pewinternet.org/2012/04/04/part-2-the-general-reading-habits-of-americans/

perspective outside of their own. Through living the experience played out in the novel, they are able to expose themselves to new ideas, experiences, and places.

But what distinguishes books that change your brain from books that don't? In Berns' description of his findings, he gives us a clue that will help us answer that question. He says that when we read stories with impactful narrative arcs our brains are changed and reorganized for at least several days. Don't you find it interesting that a neuroscientist would use literary phraseology to describe this phenomenon? What is a compelling narrative arc? Think back to chapters 4 and 6 where we discussed two of the main pillars of the first writing triangle: character and plot. In this chapter we will examine the specifics that go into both of these pillars that will compel a reader to engage with your protagonist and story and the things to avoid that readers see as lazy or uninformed writing.

You're In Trouble

One of the easiest ways to get in trouble with the reader is to neglect your research. As far as character development and setting, as a fiction writer, it is just as important to spend a sufficient amount of time and energy investigating as it is when you are writing nonfiction. Some fiction writers cling to a false (yet seemingly romantic) notion that research is for the other guy—the nonfiction writer. The problem is, when you don't get certain details just right, the experienced reader will know and feel cheated. When you assume you can put something over on another person, their intelligence comes into question. No one likes it when someone else calls them unintelligent, and that's what the writer is doing to the reader when the writer can't be bothered to get the details right.

Well, How Do I Get It Right?

At some point in the outlining process, you need to make a list of all the things you don't know about your story, characters, and setting. Then research, interview, and think things through. This list might seem intimidating, but it will save you from a world of hurt that is plausible when you publish a book without knowing all the *whys* of your story. And if you are going to have something in your story that purposefully differs from the norm, you are obligated to explain why it does within the parameters of your story. Reviews from readers that don't feel your story was true to the facts they know can be irritating because it feels like they are calling you a liar (or lazy when it comes to research). One time I had someone write to me that one of my fictional characters would have never done something like what she did because it was so unexpected. But that particular character was largely based off of me when I was preteen, and I did the thing they said was so out-of-character. At that moment, the character was fed up, as was I. I refused to change it because I knew it was possible for her to do something that extreme, but I also found that I had to explain the moment better. In my head it made instant sense, but the reader was left confused because I failed to mention that the character was at her breaking point. It is your job not to lose the reader, and sometimes that means explaining more than you want to. If there's a reason for you to do something abnormal with your character or setting, take the time to set your reader up for success in understanding what happens. You won't regret it.

Don't Assume Things Stay the Same

As time progresses, things change. That's just the

nature of the world we live in. Because of that simple and well-known fact, a lot of writers get themselves caught in a trap that makes readers doubt their dedication to their art. I'll give you a common example. Every adult has been a teenager. Growing up is a fairly universal experience. We are all born, we change and grow, and we become adults. That's part of the process of being a human. But the time period and geographical location of our teenagedom changes the way we experience it. If I am writing a period piece on teenagers of Southern California in the 90s (which I was, so it's fun to write), I can base all of the ways that the characters act, speak, and interact on my own experiences because that's where and when I grew up. But if I'm writing about characters in New York City during the 2000s, I need to interview people that experienced that city during that time so that things will be right. Reading books by other writers that lived in NYC during that time period is also a must on my prep list. Maybe not all of my readers will know what's right for that time period at that specific location, but some will, and I need to do my homework if I want to win them over. Having been a teenager isn't enough for me to be able to write about teenagers at any time period in any place. That's a trap (picture Admiral Ackbar). Always do your homework, because when you don't, readers will know and they'll be offended by your laziness. They are paying you for a product after all. It's your job to get things right.

But I Write Fantasy and/or Science Fiction, I Don't Need to Research

I will tell you right now what that heading is: an excuse. I also write both fantasy and science fiction, and there are still a ton of things I have to make sure to get right. In my YA fantasy series, one of the characters, Dawn, is mute. I've had readers tell me that they can feel her silence (and yes, I do a happy dance when I hear that). But how did that happen? Did I sit down one day and automatically knew how to write a mute character? Of course not! Listen, I'm not that smart, and neither are you. And that's okay. We can always learn more so that we write things just the way they should be. What I did to prepare for that was to think about other mute characters in books and films. I watched people. I tried out gestures and silence on my own. I watched non-verbal children interact with verbal adults. These steps were all part of my research process. Succeeding at making Dawn able to communicate without using audible words wasn't the inciting incident of my book, but without that piece of the puzzle, the entire story would have fallen apart.

As far as science fiction, I write that too (it's my true passion, though I do love helping other writers write better). When creating a fictional version of our world where space stations exist, I enlisted the help of my friend Stavros, who happens to be an architect who writes. If you can find another writer who also understands something you don't, their explanations will be next-level helpful. However, once you learn how to ask questions you need answers to, the professional you're interviewing doesn't need to be a fellow writer. I asked Stavros to imagine his reaction to getting to add a new ring to a space station I had drawn out. He asked several questions about the approach to gravity and told me part of my drawing had to be erased. Then he sat there for a moment and said, "Well, it would be a nightmare." I hadn't expected that response, so I asked why he thought that. Stavros explained that creating an entirely new section of a space station had *too* many possibilities and that any architect would find that extremely intimidating. That was the spark of information I needed in order to understand Bas Wilnis, a handsome, sharp architect, who would spearhead the ring expansion project on Bez Vonk station in my novel *Gaze at the Stars*.

Taking Your Relationship To The Next Level

When you have earned the reader's trust with high quality writing, good editing, relatable and likable characters, dynamic character arcs, and homework to assure you understand what you're writing about, you've earned something more than you probably think. In any healthy relationship, trust is key, and the same is true in your relationships with your readers. In the business world we often hear people talk about something called customer acquisition cost. What does this mean, and how is it relevant to making trusted allies out of readers?

Customer acquisition cost is the amount of money you have to pay to get one new customer for your product. In this case, your product is your book. While there are many books on how you can spend a ton of money on marketing your book, there isn't a foolproof way to get your customer acquisition cost down to $0. However, if you earn the trust of your reader, they are more prone to buy any new books just because you've written them. There are several authors that I trust so implicitly that I will always buy their new releases without even reading their book blurb. But why? How did they convince me to buy their product without paying more money to acquire my purchase through continued advertising? They are *that* good. That's it. I have read their other books, and even if I get one or two that aren't my favorite, my faith in their abilities is still high because over time they have earned my trust. For reference, three of my current favorites are Claudia Gray, Malcom Gladwell, and Charlie N. Holmberg. If any of them comes out with a book, I buy it. I have set my own alerts through BookBub to tell me when they have something new so I can buy it right away. Their cost to acquire me as a customer for any new books they come out with is $0.00 because BookBub automatically sets up "New Release" emails for any followers at no cost to the author.

Write well, invest your time and energy into something magical, and the fangirls, fanboys, and fanpeople will follow. In general, readers are one of the most loyal groups of people I have ever met. Even when a writer they love writes a dud, they will defend that author with their last breath if necessary. A good example of this is a large percentage of the fan group belonging to Andy Weir, author of *The Martian*. Before his second book, *Artemis*, even came out, people were raving about it. I went and watched him talk about it in an amazing (and life-changing, for me at least) panel at San Diego Comic Con in 2016 with other authors including Claudia Gray and James S. A. Corey. Yes, I just name-dropped. Having been in the same room as those masterful authors was a bright spot in my science fiction and fantasy writer memory. But back to *Artemis*.

As part of the big fan group that pre-ordered *Artemis*, trusting Andy's clever and inspired writing that we saw in *The Martian*, I was dejected when I figured out that the book was full of cultural insensitivity, stubborn, less-than-relatable characters, and several major plot holes. I wish he had hired me (or anyone) to be his developmental editor, because the plot had so much potential. In my despondent state, when I went on to Goodreads to write my two-star review, I noticed that there were plenty of five- and four-star reviews. I couldn't figure out why. There seemed to also be plenty of people who felt as disappointed as I did with the book. The simple truth about the diaspora between *Artemis* lovers and haters is this: people love Andy Weir, and they are going to like his book just because it has his name on it. It doesn't even need to be good. That's how dedicated book fans are. We see this phenomenon happen over and over again with other authors that don't finish a series well, or try to recreate rare and valuable writing magic. However, even dedicated fans will turn away from their favorite author after too many poorly written novels. It's also prudent to remember that cult followings don't happen to 99.9% of all authors. Choose your words carefully, always.

Content Considerations

One of the most important things to consider about your reader is the way they will react to the content inside of your book. Each genre has a target market, and that means there is data for you to contemplate. For example, if you write young adult fiction (YA), the age of your main audience ranges from fourteen to nineteen (and possibly older). That means that the language you use should be within their reading comprehension as well as their level of maturity. If you want to write something more mature as far as content, don't write YA. Because of the popularity of this genre, coupled with the desire of both authors and readers to have more mature content (think sex, swear words, and complicated life decisions), a new genre was born to accommodate this growing target audience called *new adult*. This emphasizes how important it is to get content just right.

If you are writing for children, you must research what vocabulary words are common for the age of children you're writing for. A great way to determine the level of vocabulary is to find grade-assigned spelling lists. I have three children popping about my house at any given time, so I have free access to all different levels of spelling lists, but you can use the internet to search for lists based on the age and grade level of your target audience. Look at how many syllables the words have and what type of words they are. Does the list seem adverb-happy or adjective-filled? These are the kinds of words your target age is practicing, so include as many as you like (within reason of course). But age isn't the only consideration when it comes to content decisions.

If you are writing in a specific genre, you must understand the subjects those readers will and will not prefer. For example, last year I was reading a science fiction book (big surprise), and I was surprised to be suddenly reading a scene out of a horror novel. There was blood all over the place, a giant saw, and people slumping to the floor in extensive, gory detail. First, I was eating lunch while reading this scene (lunch was ruined), and second, I was not expecting this type of content to pop up inside of a science fiction novel about artificial intelligence. It was a total put off. I had to force myself to read more of that book, and that isn't the kind of experience you want your reader (who is also your customer) to have. Remember to be considerate of your target audience's level of maturity and preference.

Inclusion and Why It Matters

In the last ten years, we have seen a surge in the inclusion movement. On behalf of both of the writers of this book, let me say how welcome and appreciated this is. Marginalized groups need representation. In order for all of us to grow as a collective of human society, we must strive to learn from experiences that are outside the realm of our own everyday lives. At the time of writing this book, there is also an unfortunate side of the inclusion movement, and that has to do with whomever inclusion is available to. What do I mean by that? Well, there are people in this world (especially on social media platforms like Facebook and Twitter) that want to tell you that unless you are transgender yourself, you shouldn't have any trangender characters in your book. In fact, if you are a white woman (like both of us are), you shouldn't be able to write any ethnic perspective aside from your own. But if only transgender writers write about transgender characters, think about how limited that type of representation in written works will be. I think this movement is extremely unfortunate because it decreases opportunities for learning and dialoguing.

Do I think that people should write from perspectives outside of their own? The answer is yes, but carefully. As we discussed in this chapter, it is extremely important for writers to do their research. Get to know someone (or several someones) who is (are) in the marginalized group you want to represent. Spend time asking them questions and learning to understand what life is like for them. Once you do your writing, give them a copy and ask them for feedback. If you're still worried that you haven't gotten it right, go hire a sensitivity reader—a person whose job it is to make sure the group you're trying to represent won't be offended by incorrect stereotypes or uninformed language. When I write men, I bug my husband to no end with questions and then I have him check and double-check everything. He is so sweet and helps me a lot, but imagine what my male characters would sound like without his input. I imagine they would come off as significantly more female than they ought to (not that there can't be more sensitive and emotionally concerned variations of masculinity, but certainly not all men are that way). Always do your research.

A Note On Race

Don't panic. I already told you I'm white, didn't I? Maybe you think I'm not qualified to write about how to write about race. Well, in this case, I completely agree. But I can point you in the direction of one source which I have found immensely helpful when thinking about writing characters that are of a race outside of my own. There is an amazing and exhaustive Tumblr about writing diverse characters called 'Writing With Color[4],' written by four helpful and compassionate women: Colette, Alice, Jessica, and Leysa. I recommend you spend several days reading through all of their posts and suggestions. You will be a much better writer for it. On their homepage they remind their reader (in this case, you) that if you've decided it's too easy to get writing diverse characters wrong, you're making a decision to reject inclusion because you are afraid. Making choices based on fear is always a bad idea. If you made the choice to write, you have to overcome fear on an intense level, but don't stop there. Keep going. Your readers will appreciate it, and remember that ultimately, one of your goals as a writer is to turn new readers into a loyal fan base.

Expensive Words

Have you ever read a book that resonated within your very soul? I guarantee that the words you read to get there cost that author something. I have a theory that spending part of yourself when you write leads to more meaningful and impactful stories. I think about this theory whenever I'm writing something that makes my stomach churn or makes me cry. Some of the most painful experiences in my life have been poured into my

---

[4] https://writingwithcolor.tumblr.com

characters, plots, and books in the form of tears tied to outpouring words. In the middle of writing *Gaze at the Stars*, my science fiction Romance stand-alone, my father-in-law died from complications due to a skiing accident. The sudden loss of one of the most influential people in my life wrecked me. I didn't know how I would ever write again. Today, I was looking at the photos of him around my house, and I still can't believe he's gone. When I finally felt like I was ready to start writing again, one of the plot points in *Gaze* suddenly stuck out to me more than anything else, the fact that Stijn Erlie, the father of the protagonist, had died, and (mini spoiler) Shaul finds out that his father recorded a message before Stijn's sudden death.

Once I had gone through something similar to what I had written into Shaul's life, I realized that something like that would have affected Shaul in such a huge way, that his grief would have poured over into other huge moments in his life. In fact, Shaul himself was a writer, and I knew that his experiences should show through in *Shaul's* writing as well. The result is a scene where Shaul writes about a character seeing someone in the space station that looks like his father, and falling under a tidal wave of emotions once he realizes that the familiar-looking figure cannot possibly be the man he loves that he lost. This story was based on my own experience after seeing a man with the same-shaped, mostly-bald head as my father-in-law at the airport, and realizing, once again, that I would never see my father-in-law on this side of heaven.

The best way for you to connect with your readers is to be as transparent as possible. If you can stand it, use your own emotions and experiences as fuel for your writing. If you can't stand it, figure out how to get there. I promise it will change your writing forever.

Because I own the rights to *Gaze* I can share it with you here. There isn't a better way I can think of to end this chapter. I hope the expensive words show.

No One to Blame
Zan looked out as the ebb and flow of people moving through the spaceport created an asymmetrical wave. Then it happened. His heart raved. Hope soared through his entire body, from the tip of his big toenail to the tip of the longest strand of hair on his head. But then he remembered.

The rush of hope pulsing through his veins was quickly followed by bile rising up his throat. Of course it wasn't him. That wasn't possible. His father was dead. But the man who was now scuttling out of the area with a small bag slung over his shoulder had looked so much like his father from behind. It was a combination of the man's thin build, soft bald spot, the way he moved, and tan skin. Or maybe it was all wishful thinking. But the familiar tick that tricked his brain into believing the impossible wasn't his father's. It belonged to a stranger.

He was in a sophisticated can filled with a precise mixture of gases that sustained human life. A buzz, starting out low and transitioning to a high-pitched shrill, filled up the spaces in his ears and in his thoughts. If only he could remember the way his father laughed. The sound of his voice. The way the timber of his voice changed when he told Zan he loved him. Every time this happened, it was as if he had lost his father all over again. He had to snap out of it, or he was going to pass out.

Expensive thoughts. The memories cost him every time. He would need to sleep for a day and a half after this. But he was willing to pay the price. To acknowledge that his father was alive, but now he was dead. He couldn't figure out anyone to blame.

It had been a blood clot. Something unpreventable, according to the doctors. It didn't matter if they had known it existed. It still would have killed him.

Zan shook his head back and forth in an attempt to shake off the tears that threatened to break free. Maybe he would be the guy someone caught passing out at the airport. Some streaming vid people watched for a minute of entertainment. But so what? He let the tears come. Everyone told him to ride the wave. Let it pass. But there were waves that never let you feel like you've ridden them all the way to the edge of the shore.

One of Zan's greatest regrets was that his father never saw him as a man. He would never be a grandfather to his hypothetical children. His father wouldn't be there for the celebrations, the births, the other deaths. And he had already missed Zan graduating from high school, then college, the day Zan found out he was finally getting a job he actually liked. There was joy in all of those moments, but also the pain of knowing he couldn't share them with the man who helped shape who he had become. The duality was familiar, but familiarity didn't kill his pain. It didn't lessen the sharpness of the razor's edge. His soul was bleeding, again. It was almost as if he could watch the blood drip down, pooling into a puddle on the spaceport floor. He still couldn't figure out who to blame.

He looked up and spotted an elderly woman.

She walked over to him and set her hand on his arm. "Why don't I help you to a seat."

"I'm fine," Zan said.

He didn't mean it. The woman must have known that. She kept guiding him. When he was safely in his chair, she sat across from him.

"Two bits for your thoughts?"

"My dad," Zan whispered. If he spoke at normal volume the knot in his throat was going to burst.

"Sick?"

"Dead."

"How long?"

"Years."

"You were just a boy, then?"

"Yes."

"I'm so sorry," she said. "I have that look on my face more days than not. It always stings, doesn't it? No matter how long it's been?"

"Who?"

"My daughter. Barb. Suicide. She wasn't well." Tears pooled in her eyeballs as their whites turned pink.

"I'm sorry," Zan said. Though his gut told him he should be embarrassed, a grown man nearly fainting at the airport because of a random stranger that looked like his dad, but the understanding in her gaze told his gut to shut up.

She looked down at her hands. "It's hard. Something bad happens... or something good. You want to go to them, ask them what they think. But the best you can do is replay the things they said—if you can remember —and retell them to yourself. And even though your voice sounds kind of like their voice, it's not the same. And you'll never see the joy in their eyes when they look at you again. But there isn't anyone to blame, really, is there?"

A loud speaker came on. "Now boarding, flight 30ab2 to Earth."

"That's me," the woman said.

"Long flight," Zan said.

"Yes, I'm not looking forward to it, but I can't wait to see my son and my grandbaby."

"Safe trip," Zan said. "And thanks."

"Here's my number, if you ever need to talk." The woman tapped her wrist terminal to Zan's. The name Queenie Gregs came up with her message information.

"My name's Zan. See you, Queenie."

"Nice to meet you, Zan."

He knew the thrill of empathy. It was a shock to his grief that seemed to smooth out all the jagged edges.

Once in a while, it would happen. He would meet someone who understood. The tears in their eyes matched the tears in his. The familiarity didn't take away the pain—a theme he noticed developing. But knowing someone else understood was a balm over the scabbed-over cuts in his soul. He would cry with the empathizer, wordless tears speaking multitudes. But in an instant, it would be over.

Zan watched Queenie walk away. His friend was waiting. He had to get back to his life. The one he knew his father had wanted him to live, even if that meant he had to go on without him. So he did. And he was sad. But sad wasn't just a feeling anymore. It was something he wore. He could never take it off. And there wasn't anyone to blame.

CHAPTER 9

BOOK SERVICES: THE HELP YOU NEED BUT MIGHT NOT WANT

When I first started my writing career, I was completely broke. I was living in a country other than my homeland, and was not allowed to seek employment. At some point, I may have had to eat produce someone else had accidentally dropped into the gutter, and to also feed that gutter-inspired chili and potatoes to my children. It was a humbling moment. But the simple truth is, I didn't have any money available for book services. When it came to having my first book edited, I called in all the favors I could. My friend Rachel was working as an editor, so she read through part of it during her time off of work. Another friend, Sarah, was going through a Master's program in England, so we were on the same time zone and she had been writing her own papers non-stop. She spent half of her vacation time in Greece with my manuscript and a red pen in hand. Having a good support group helps when you're attempting any endeavor. However, upon hiring a professional editor this year to finally fix my first book, I can tell you that there were still a ton of notes and corrections. Why? Because my friends were either too inexperienced to edit it properly, or they had the qualifications but were too busy with paying jobs to finish editing my project for free.

In this chapter, we will look at the various book services available to you, and discuss what you can skip (and when), what you absolutely can never skip (though you can do some bargain shopping), and how to use hybrid hiring approaches to get the laymen labor done cheap while saving every penny you can to utilize a talented book services professional for the complicated stuff.

Understanding Professional Services in General

Spring is coming! Let's say you hire a landscaping designer to do some work around your yard. You're looking for a curb appeal update and easy-to-maintain yard systems. He says, "No problem. I charge $40 an hour. Does that sound good to you?" You respond a resounding yes, excited for your house to finally look habitable. There are a zillion weeds outside that need to go away, yesterday. Dreams of lounging on your covered porch while gazing at your pristine yard fill your head. You can all but hear the happy birds singing their predictable springtime songs. But when the landscaper gives you a bill for $200, $120 more than you were expecting, your heart drops. Then he hands you a plan, and before you can even poke your head out of the door you realize that the weeds are still happily in place. You realize you won't be going to the mall to get a new spring outfit after all. But what happened? And what do weeds have to do with copyediting?

The first thing you have to do with any professional

services provider is educate yourself on what their job is. In the case of the not-so-landscaped yard, you hired a landscaping designer to create and implement systems when what you really wanted was a gardener to pull your weeds and refer some water-saving plants for your area that you can put in your yard. You didn't understand what service you were paying for. This relates to copyediting in the way that writers that haven't used one before don't understand exactly what a copyeditor does, and what services are comprised by their hourly rate. Let's look at the different types of editing according to where the process happens in the book-creation timeline.

Developmental Editing: Making Sure You Get It Right

What is a developmental editor? That is a great question, and surprisingly few people know the answer. Kristin, our in-house developmental editor, has to explain what her job is to everyone she meets, but we're hoping to put an end to that for every person who reads this book.

de·vel·op·men·tal ed·i·tor /dəˌveləpˈmen(t)l/ /ˈedədər/ *noun*
the first stop in the editing journey. someone who loves writing and reading equally and is on a quest to make every novel they work with the best possible version of itself even if that means they have to push the writer to make changes. an expert in all genre tropes and expectations who keeps up with the industry trends and standards. an individual that

understands what keeps readers reading and what makes them stop. also known as a book doctor in the traditional publishing industry. a writer's best friend. professional storyteller.

Now that we know the definition, it is important to note that not every manuscript needs a developmental editor (DE). But before you decide whether or not to employ one, you first need to understand what a developmental editor does. DEs have a lot of big and tiny things to think about when they're going through your manuscript. For example, let's say that you are writing a memoir and want to resonate with a certain audience. You wouldn't just hire any developmental editor because they might not specialize in nonfiction. You need to find someone who can help you take your project in combination with your target audience and create a product that will be well received. This doesn't mean that you have a happy ending or that you tick off all of the expectation boxes your target audience has, but that you have done enough hard work to assure that your book will be something that will stay with the reader mentally long after they have finished reading it. Remember, a successful author can make the reader feel the way the author wants the reader to feel for good or for bad. A developmental editor understands the nuances behind accomplishing that task.

If you're already hungry, you might want to take a quick break and grab something to eat, because now we're going to talk about something important/delicious: stew. The trick to making a good stew is to start with the best ingredients possible. If you're using meat, you pay for something nice and then you brown all of the sides in a pan before you add the pieces to the stew. If you're looking for something vegetarian or vegan, you look for fresh, local produce. The things you put into the stew help create something that is either amazing, or bland. You think about spices, broths, and preparation methods. Should you sweat the onions or add them into the broth raw? And then, once you have determined all of the other stew-making methodology you want to use, you add in one more factor: time.

Developmental editors are the stew makers of the writing world. First, they ascertain your writing goals. Second, they take an inventory of all of your ingredients: characters, plot, setting, tone, voice, consistency in any one of those areas, imagery, etcetera. As they read through your manuscript, they evaluate these ingredients to see what kind of quality they possess. Then they look at your cooking methods. How is it that you've combined everything? Does this combination create a stew that would taste good to your target audience? Does it accomplish all of the goals you wanted to meet when you started this project? If the answer to either of the last two questions is "no" they will give you suggestions on what you could change to meet your goals. Good developmental editors will even argue with their clients when the client is tired and doesn't want to make any more changes. Exhaustion is not a good excuse to come just close of achieving your goals, and DEs who really care about the project know how to motivate the writer to give all they have in exchange of creating a manuscript that accomplishes everything it was meant to achieve.

Are you unsure of your manuscript's ability to live up to your idea's potential? Have you gotten 3/4ths of the way through your story and gotten stuck? Are you unsure of what your target audience expects or how to subvert those expectations in a welcomed manner? A developmental editor will be a great help to you. To find a helpful developmental editor who is excited to work with you, you can check out these websites: the Editorial Freelances Association for a referral (the-efa.com), BookBaby (bookbaby.com), Reedsy (reedsy.com), or Literary Symmetry (literarysymmetry.com).

Copyediting: Word to the Wordsmith

What does a copyeditor do? They go through your manuscript one line at a time—and a good copyeditor will do this at least two times (which in editor language is referred to as two passes)—noting grammatical and spelling mistakes, errors in usage, confusing passages, and inconsistent style. Some will note confusing passages for you to fix while others will fix them for you, but before you hire someone you should ask them about what price covers what edits. Though from the outside, copyediting seems like a rather simple endeavor, it can become endless and costly quickly. Let's examine why as we look at the different levels of copyediting.

Levels of Copyediting

One of the main factors in editorial pricing is time. The more hours that are required to create a clean manuscript, the more money is involved. Because of this, publishers and editors offer various levels of editing so that if there is a tight budget, an edit is still possible. Though every editor would no doubt love to be able to do a heavy edit on every manuscript to make it into its best possible self, editors understand that money is not an unlimited resource. In response to this issue, there are three levels of editing from which you can choose: light, medium, and heavy. They increase in both expense and coverage from left to right. The important thing to remember is to ask each editor what their versions of these levels include. Then you have to determine what you can afford and how much help your manuscript needs. If you have left a ton of errors and inconsistencies in your manuscript, a good copyeditor won't agree to a light copyedit because it would either be left full of errors, or they would be working extra hours for free. Always make sure to work with an editor that asks for a sample so that they can give you an accurate estimate (more on pricing later).

Don't Make Assumptions
It used to be that a copyeditor would automatically count everything that needed counting and make sure the numbers added up in the end. For example, Tasha starts out with five vials of antiflatulence medicine in her bag. She's going on a day-long interview three hours away and doesn't want her digestion issues to create a foul first impression. Halfway through the short story, she has taken three, but magically has three left. That doesn't work, does it? An editor would make a note that if she has taken three, there should only be two left in her bag. I have recently heard from other writers that not all copyeditors are providing this level of detailed editing, but in our opinion, they should. Double check with the editor you are considering about this *before* you sign a contract.

The Process
After your editor writes queries (questions about your content and/or style choices), you will respond with a file where you have accepted and rejected suggestions and answered queries. At this point, you will usually have to pay for a third and final pass of your manuscript (which we recommend). If you don't want to address any of your choices with your editor at this point and you are self-published, you can skip ahead to getting your manuscript formatted and then hire a proofreader, but remember that if you make changes after you've already paid for your manuscript to be formatted, you

will have to pay your formatter a second time.

That brings us to another aspect of working with a copyeditor: the contract. One of the most difficult things that copyeditors deal with is time management, but not their own. Writers are often tempted to endlessly tweak their manuscripts, opting to turn them in to their copyeditors late. A normal copyediting process for a manuscript around 50,000 to 100,000 words takes from two to four weeks. If a copyeditor has their next six to twelve months booked, and one person is even two weeks late, it creates an unfortunate domino effect that impacts the experience of every customer down the line. That is why many copyeditors will either charge a late fee for the extra hours they won't be able to spend with their families, or reserve the right to completely drop a client that hasn't turned in their manuscript on time.

Finding An Editor That Appreciates Your Voice

Before you get the actual hiring process, I want to encourage you to think about something specific when looking for an editor to work with. Depending on the genre and style of your book, you will develop a certain voice. This is part of the writing process, but unfortunately, not all editors will seek to maintain your carefully cultivated voice. If you find an editor who nitpicks your manuscript to death over things that are grammatically acceptable, or is changing things for a purpose other than ease of understanding, it may be time to find a different editor. You need to hire someone who understands your vision and voice because otherwise they will change things that don't need to be changed, or correct things in such a way that they will seem disjointed to the reader. A great way to discover whether or not your editor cares about your voice is to ask *why* changes appear that don't seem necessary or that don't flow with the voice you've created. If their answers are curt and lack sufficient explanation, it is likely that the editor you're working with doesn't care about your voice. If you receive a detailed explanation with careful language, you will know that your editor is on your team and is working to maintain your voice.

Investing In Your Manuscript

Hiring a copyeditor is really a specific form of investing in your manuscript. It's not just money. It's money spent to create a better product that you will be selling for years. That is an investment. If you like the idea of having passive income, think about how much more passive income you could earn if you avoid getting reviews that say things like "Too many typos, distracting" or "Could have used more editing." But now that you're convinced you need a copyeditor, how much do they cost?

The quick answer is that the industry standard for copyeditors is $35 an hour. The price can add up fast when you submit something to an editor that needs a heavy copyedit. This type of manuscript has several qualities that make copyeditors want to scream, such as no punctuation, no capitalization of any words, confusing sentences, too many adverbs, no adverbs at all, no understanding of basic grammar, plot holes, and plot and character inconsistencies. Be forewarned, if you submit a manuscript that has all (or even a few) of these issues, you are going to pay to have them fixed. The best thing you can do is to submit a properly polished manuscript to an editor, so that they will only have to do a medium or light copyedit. Less time on their part equals less money spent on your part. But how do you polish your manuscript? And when is too much polishing detrimental?

Polishing Your Manuscript

The methods I am going to suggest to help you polish

your manuscript are not new. These ideas have been tested by both writers and editors for decades. Feel free to experiment and find out what approach best helps you to see your manuscript with fresh eyes.

-Once you finish your first draft, take a break from it. A total break. If you think about something you might want to change, write it down in a separate document or in a notebook. Do not go back to your original document and start changing things.

-While we recommend taking at least three weeks away from working on your work in progress (also known as a WIP), there are some that feel two weeks of break time is enough. We strongly recommend a month. Take that month to start researching which book services professionals you might want to work with, but don't email or call them yet. You still have some work to do before you're ready for that step.

-When you start your first round of edits (we usually do four or five rounds on our own projects), use a different font than what you wrote in. It will make the words look and feel different, which is what you need. You can also change the background in your document to a different color, or if you prefer to do your first round of edits with a pen and paper, print out your manuscript on colored paper. Pastel colors work best.

-Don't keep editing the same section. Give yourself a daily word goal and keep plowing through. If you find plot holes, note them in a second document along with the places that need to be changed. One useful thing about software is that you can search within the document for different words. Note three to four words in a row of where you need to come back so that when you search, you only have one or two results. If you note the section as "chapter three, 'she ran'" you might run into several sections that use those words and figuring out which one you need to adjust sucks away valuable editing time.

–Take a week off of editing (it's a great idea to have multiple projects in various stages so you can switch to something else and still be productive, though you should avoid writing the first drafts of new projects at the same time). Then go back and fix all of the things you noted in your first round of edits. Address the character and plot problems you found.

–When you finish the second round of edits, send your manuscript to an alpha reader. An alpha reader is *not* a friend of yours who says they like to read. The person you choose as an alpha reader should be familiar with the expectations and tropes of your genre and actually be committed to getting through your manuscript in a timely manner (let's say two weeks). If you don't already know someone who fits those criteria, consider searching around on Twitter. It's a great resource for writers and readers. Make sure to use *#alphareader* and *#writingcommunity* in your tweet. While they are reading, get started on your third draft.

–Change the font and paper/document color again. Now look for confusing passages or typos. Make sure to work through the entire manuscript again, using a daily word goal. Your bones are good and you've done the hard work of fixing plot holes. It's time to start focusing on the minor issues.

–Do a fourth draft with input from your alpha reader, and start sending out emails to potential editors to find out what their schedules look like.

–Get ready to turn in your finished fourth draft to an

editor. Don't keep editing it. At this point you will definitely have what writers and editors call "mistake blindness." No matter how many more times you go through your manuscript, you won't be able to see any more mistakes.

Congratulations, you've got a pre-polished manuscript that will allow your editor to work quickly.

<u>Bargain Shopping for an Editor</u>

While many copyeditors charge per hour, there are several editing companies or co-ops that offer estimates based on the state and length of your manuscript. For example, at our company, Literary Symmetry (literarysymmetry.com), we offer light copyediting for pre-polished manuscripts that equate to much less than $35 an hour. We do this because as writers ourselves, we understand that while editing is a must, most new writers can't afford the standard industry fee.

If you're looking for a more traditional approach to copyediting pricing, you can ask the Editorial Freelances Association for a referral (the-efa.com) or look at established book services providers like BookBaby (bookbaby.com) or Reedsy (reedsy.com) where you can submit your information for a price quote.

No matter which approach you choose, never forget the triangle law. When hiring a professional, there are usually three things to consider, like the angles of a triangle. These angles are comprised of quality, speed, and affordability. At any given time, you can have two of these, but never all three. So, if you find an editor who's willing to take on your urgent project for a fraction of the price other professionals are asking, beware, for the editing might be sloppy.

<u>Copyediting's Fraternal Twin: Proofreading</u>

Proofreading is an additional paid option that most book services professionals offer. The way that proofreading differs from copyediting is that it is meant to be a final pass to look for any mistakes that have been left in the manuscript after copious amounts of editing have already taken place. Copyediting happens before the book has been formatted. Proofreading happens after everything has been formatted into its final, publishable form. In the case of proofreading, the editor won't usually do three passes through your manuscript. Because of the fact that proofreading is supposed to come after copyediting, proofreading is usually less expensive. If you are going to self-publish, this is something you should at least think about. You can see the list of options available earlier in this chapter, as the same places also offer proofreading services.

Cover Design: Yes, They Will Judge Your Book By Its Cover

We know we've already said that you must pay for a copyeditor, and that's true. But you must also pay for a cover designer. Even if you have some graphic design experience, the way that a book cover is designed takes several important knowledge bases and throws them together to create something that looks nice, reads easily, and markets the content. If you don't have experience in publishing, graphic design, and marketing, it's best for you to look for someone else that does. The most important thing that your cover does is communicate with your reader. If they don't find the cover appealing, they won't read your book description. To paraphrase James Patterson's words, a book won't sell if it doesn't get picked up.

A lot of authors think that a weak cover is fine as long as their book is in the correct category listing because the description will tell the buyer all they need to know, but that isn't the case. This is especially true when readers are searching for books online because they don't even see the description on book-selling websites during a product search. In fact, all web browsers see when they search for books on retailers like Amazon or Barnes & Noble is the cover. As readers, we can both vouch for the truth of the situation that people definitely judge books by their covers. If the cover isn't attention-grabbing, it's almost like the book doesn't exist at all.

<u>Whom Should I Hire?</u>
There is a ton of different options for hiring cover designers. You can go on Fiverr (fiverr.com) and pay anywhere from $10 to $300. You can also go on Google and search for "Affordable Cover Design." Whatever approach you take, whether it's asking a cover designing friend or calling up an old high school flame who was known for being artsy, here are three questions that will help you determine if the designer you're thinking about knows anything about designing book covers.

1. What will you do to make sure that people who are viewing my book cover on a Kindle, Nook, or smart phone screen will be able to get the maximum impact from my cover?
The Correct Answer is:
Make sure that both the title and author name are easy to read even when the image is in thumbnail form.
But why?

Experienced book cover designers don't just think about the impact of the cover, they also think about the purpose. Your cover is your single most important marketing lead. If the designer hasn't thought about how your cover will read in thumbnail form, they don't understand the industry. This is why the font selection and size of your title and author name are so vital. You want people to be able to read your cover no matter how big or small it appears on the screen in front of them.

2. Can you take these five images I downloaded from some photo site and make them into one cohesive cover?
The Correct Answer is:
No.
But why?
This is a classic mistake a lot of "cover designers" make when they are trying too hard to please their client. It is their job to know what would look best on the cover. Five images (or even two) shot at different times with different shadows will automatically look wrong to the human eye. An experienced designer will tell you that they can combine the two concepts you like, but not using two different stock photos (unless those two photos are separated by some type of color block or border in the middle). They might also offer to make the art from scratch, which will cost you more, but will most definitely be

worth the extra money.

3. Will you do unlimited edits on my cover if I pay you one time?

The Correct Answer is:

No... but I'll give you three edits (or something like that).

But why?

Listen, if you find someone willing to do unlimited edits, that means they must not be very good at their job because they are putting in time, and at some point that time doesn't equal any more money. Also, authors don't know how to design book covers (or they wouldn't pay someone else to do it) and if they demand endless edits, they risk ruining the cover with too many specific change requests. If you aren't sure that the designer you are working with will get it right the first time, it is reasonable to ask for two variations of your cover to choose from. However, it is unprofessional (and in bad taste) to ask anyone to work for free. When you ask for unlimited edits, that is essentially what you are doing.

Our advice is to send out these three questions to any cover designer you are considering, along with a request to see two or three book covers they have designed for other books in your genre.

Paperback File vs. Digital Cover

There are different types of files you will need for your book cover depending on which media the book is being released on. For paperback covers, there is a lot more work than those that are digital (and Amazon has gotten really picky about these files lately), so there is more cost involved. To create a file for a hardback book there is even more work (think book jackets). Make sure you communicate with your designer what your cover needs are so they can quote you the appropriate prices for each format.

Interior Formatting: The Final Frontier of Formatting

So you've finished the final draft of your book and had it edited by a professional? Awesome! You have persevered, but now what? You already know that you need to hire someone to create a cover, but what about the formatting of the inside of your book? If you don't know what it means to format the interior of your book, go grab a paperback (or hardback) and then open your favorite ebook reading device. Do you see how the letters, words, chapter headings, and paragraphs are arranged? That's interior formatting. And the best thing about this type of formatting is that, in general, you don't need to pay anyone to do it.

Whether you use Microsoft Word, Scrivener, Ulysses, or Vellum to write your books, there are options through all of these softwares to format your files into ebook form. We use Scrivener, which was less than $30 with a coupon given to those who successfully did 50,000 words in November through a certain awesome organization that has a trademarked name. The first problem with Scrivener is that there isn't really a way to learn to use it to format other than paid tutorials. The second problem is that the software engineers are constantly changing things in a way that doesn't make the user experience any easier. Maybe the two major problems sound like a drawback, but the benefit is that you can create your own templates for both ebooks and print PDFs from the file in the same software where you've written your manuscript. That makes editing simpler in that you don't have to go back and forth between two different files like we used to have to do back in the day when our only really customizable print formatting option was Adobe InDesign. Vellum and Ulysses also offer the option to format your print-ready PDF and ebook from the same file, but we can't really offer advice using these two different software options because we stick with Scrivener (for now... we're looking at you, whoever took the "Page Break" option away from the Inspector).

But paid software isn't your only viable option. If you're looking for totally free file formatting, you can use Draft2Digital (draft2digital.com) or Reedsy (reedsy.com/write-a-book). Just know that whatever you choose, there will be a learning curve. There are several hundred videos on YouTube about how to format your book using X, Y, or Z, so make sure to do some searching around on the interwebs before you start formatting.

Pay Me My Money

You can also choose to skip over this possibly infuriating process by paying someone to do interior formatting for you. There are options that go for as little as $10 on Fivver. Remember that with these deals, you get what you pay for. You can also pay upwards of $300 for custom print-ready PDF files. It's up to you. If you are going to hire a designer to create a formatted file for you, make sure to ask for samples of their past work and ask about how much it would be for them to make edits if you find typos later (which happens with almost every book in existence).

But I Want to be Traditionally Published

If your goal is to have your manuscript traditionally published, there are still advantages to using every single one of these services. For example, if you want to have a better chance of an agent picking up your manuscript, the cleaner it is, the better. It is also important to know how to format your book into some sort of file because you will still want to send it to alpha and beta readers to get input. If your book has been requested based on the query you've written, but not optioned, it means that while your premise is intriguing, there must be something off in the first few chapters. At this point, a developmental editor might be valuable to you.

<u>What Does it Mean to Query?</u>

To query means that you submit a query of your manuscript, play, or book of poetry to book industry professionals, called book agents, who would act as a go-between for you and publishing companies. A query is a specific document you create to share with book agents containing all of the pertinent information they need to know about your book. When an agent is interested in a query, they will usually request a certain number of the first chapters of your book to investigate whether your manuscript is a fit for any of the publishers they work with. Though it is no longer regularly updated, Query Shark is a wonderful resource to learn to write a query and can be found at queryshark.blogspot.com.

CHAPTER 10

BONUS: TROPES AND TARGETS

To celebrate both the new cover of *Write the Perfect Read - The Fiction Edition* and the audio book release, we decided to add a bonus chapter about tropes and target audience expectations that will help you go further in your writing journey. While these two ideas are not necessarily part of the bigger picture of what the six pillars are, you will still need to understand them if you want any chance of being able to pitch or sell your story. So, let's get started, shall we?

The Triumphant Trope

Many writers hear the word "trope" and start to feel dirty. But why? And what is a trope? Let's define it first, and then we'll explain why some writers treat it like a bad word.

trope /trōp/ *noun*
An important and often commonly occurring theme or motif. Certain tropes are often identified as belonging to a certain genre of creative work. A *literary trope* can refer to the use of a word, image, or phrase that represents artistic meaning within a work to achieve a certain goal.

The idea of what a trope is might seem complicated, so let's look at an example most of us are familiar with: the hero's journey.

One of my favorite hero's journey type stories is *Pilgrim's Progress* by John Bunyan. I can relate to Christian, the main character. He goes on a journey to get rid of the burden that weighs him down, even though his family thinks he is crazy. He learns that his city is going to be destroyed, and tries to warn his family, but to no avail. The idea of the hero's journey is part of a widely known, and reader-expected trope. Christian receives a call to go on an adventure. At this point he is forced to choose to either abandon his family or to give up on his journey, which is the beginning, or threshold of his adventure. Next, he has to go through several trials, which in his case, equates to meeting different characters who promise him he doesn't need to go on this journey to get rid of his burden. There is a descent into the death/rebirth portion of his story as he faces almost impossible situations (at one point he literally falls into a pit called Slough of Despond). Then he starts to find characters and paths that support his upward journey toward The Celestial City, but even after he finally gets rid of his burden, he learns there is another challenging set of things he must do to successfully journey to The Celestial City. As Christian passes through the temptations and challenges he faces along the way, he changes. Finally, he is faced with the last obstacle, overcomes it, and is able to enter into The Celestial City with his new companion, Hope. In most versions of stories that employ the hero's journey trope, the hero returns home changed, but in this case, Christian realizes he is now in his new home. His hero's journey is complete.

I'm sure you can think of many instances of this trope. A few famous examples aside from *Pilgrim's Progress* are *The Lord of the Rings* series, *Star Wars* (the original trilogy covers Luke Skywalker's journey while the prequels show us the beginning of Anakin Skywalker's journey which is completed in the original trilogy), and even something as simple (yet awesome) as a *Curious George* book. But if tropes are so common that we can find the same trope, like the hero's journey, in large-scale fantasy book series, epic film trilogies, and even children's stories, why do some people think they are so cringe-worthy?

There is a theory floating around that if something is popular, it must not be clever or creative. And that is why some writers and readers complain about tropes. The ideas are *too* familiar, they argue. But what this minority of thinkers doesn't understand is that if your book is *too* unfamiliar, readers, viewers, or listeners get mad. They have certain expectations they assume will be met, because certain tropes are expected in certain genres. When these expectations are not met, the audience feels cheated. For example, think of a hero's journey where the hero dies halfway through their hero track. Does that sound anticlimactic? That's because it is. How would you feel if a writer made you care about a character to just kill them, without any purpose? If that happened to me as a reader I would be mad because that writer wasted my time. There is a reason that tropes become tropes in the first place: because they work. But can you be clever and creative while using a trope?

The simple answer to whether an author can make

creative art while using a popular trope is: yes. There are endless ways in which a writer can tweak and even subvert trope expectations to the pure delight of the reader. In the example we looked at of the hero's journey, we observed how at the end of Christian's journey, he doesn't go home. First of all, he can't, because his home has been destroyed. But also, why would he want to go back there when he can stay in The Celestial City? John Bunyan adjusted the trope to make sense with the story he was writing, but his ending also gives the reader the same sense of closure that happens at the typical end of the hero's journey loop when the protagonist returns home. This proves that as long as we find a way to satisfy every expected action within a trope, we don't have to write tropes verbatim. But, if we skip part of the expected trope altogether without a substitute, our readers will feel dissatisfied, and their reviews and allegiances will reflect that.

Genre-Specific Tropes

In each genre, there are trope expectations that every reader will bring into your story with them as they begin to read. In faerie fantasy, the readers are familiar with the outsider/savior trope. Some half-faerie, half-human character appears at the beginning of the story, and usually, that character also happens to be the savior that will preserve the magic of nature for generations to come. So, if you have a protagonist who is half-faerie and half-human and has nothing to do with the preservation of faerie life or the preservation of magic, that is going to throw off your faerie fantasy reader. The outsider/savior trope is familiar to them, and if you give them a hint that you will be employing this trope, they will be actively searching for it. And, if you don't have a good reason for subverting that trope expectation (and no, "I didn't feel like it" isn't a good reason), then you are going to have an irritated reader. You do not want to irritate the reader. If you have a clever way to subvert this trope expectation, however, the reader will be glad to go along with you on this trope-breaking journey.

The popular half-human, half-faerie protagonist outsider/savior trope is one that Julie Kawagawa subverted in an expert manner by giving the main character in her *Iron Fey* series powers that seem contradictory to saving nature, as these powers are more aligned with technology. The result is a best-selling series that fulfilled the trope desires of the reader without seeming boring and redundant by doing so. It's like when you watch the same kind of show, over and over again, because you like that type of show. Let's use a superhero show as an example. You're watching a new superhero drama and, so far, it has fulfilled all of the normal hero trope expectations. But, then one day, something in the show seems out of place but also exciting at the same time. Maybe it turns out that the villain is actually a kind-of good guy and teams up with the hero to defeat an even bigger villain. Your expectation is fulfilled by the show, but the show-runners also teach you that you have the ability to like something that doesn't necessarily follow the same cookie-cutter writing that the other superhero shows follow.

The faerie outsider/savior and the superhero-versus-villain tropes are just two of many that readers find familiar. And now that we are more consciously aware of the existence of these types of tropes, we must ask ourselves what tropes readers will expect to see in our chosen genres. For example, I've been researching what different space fantasy and science-fiction time-travel tropes are common so that I can employ these tropes in my own fiction writing. I know these tropes, because I am also a fangirl of these genres myself. However, I had never previously gone through and broken down the steps within these genre-popular tropes until I was interested in writing them. I was vaguely conscious of the tropes as fan, but I needed to become super aware of these tropes if I wanted to not only include them in my own stories, but also successfully subvert them in a way that the reader will find satisfying. And I also wanted to learn what the current market demand for specific tropes is, because that will affect my book sales. (A great book on understanding market-friendly tropes is *Write to Market: Deliver a Book that Sells* by Chris Fox.) My research has taught me that if I want to write a time-travel story, I should probably have a door to a different time (and/or dimension), and that within this door, I should have a new (and probably prehistoric) cultural dimension that my protagonist will have to adapt to so that when the right time comes, he (and it should probably be a he) will save this group of people from an outside threat so that he can finally get back through the time-door, where meaningful relationships with his family or love interest wait to be restored. But why this trope? Is it new? Why do readers like it right now?

The thing I want you to understand is that trope popularity changes over time, constantly. It's always in flux, because reader preferences are also always adapting and changing. But, the same tropes rotate into popularity over and over again, and if you can predict which tropes will rotate into popularity next (or be one of the first ones to notice a new rotation) then your books will not only sell well, but earn you loyal fans. The time-travel/prehistoric trope isn't new. In fact, it's quite old. You can read books by Arthur Conan Doyle or C. S. Lewis that tackle this trope (and I have). But their sudden resurgence is something I noticed in current indie books, and the sales of stories containing these tropes are currently soaring. I'm sure you've started to notice a theme developing as I describe my research and trope knowledge: it was acquired through a lot of reading. That's right, as a writer, you need to read. We discussed that earlier in the book, but now, you can see one of the big reasons why reading is so important to the writer.

If you're going to successfully figure out which tropes belong to your genre of stories and which ones are fading in and out of present popularity, you need to read. And in order to best choose which books to read, you need to find ones that fit into your preferred mode of publishing. If you're going indie, find other indie books in your genre that are performing well for consistent lengths of time. Take screenshots of the top twenty in the genre on Amazon and compare them over time. Make sure that all of the books you're keeping track of are also indie, which you can determine on Amazon by the fact that they will not specifically mention any publisher information (which has changed three times since I started adding this section of the bonus chapter, so I made a webpage you can check for up-to-date information at literarysymmetry.com/howcanitell). If you're going to shoot for traditional publishing, this is a bit more difficult because from what I can tell, publishers aren't as interested in tropes and marketing trends, but if you pay attention to which stories are doing consistently well and note what tropes they have employed, this should help. But don't go after the obvious choices, because there will be too much competition due to an oversaturated market; like when a million vampire books came out after the *Twilight Series* became a smash hit but very few of them sold. And remember, if you're going to subvert a popular trope, just make sure you fill in the part you're replacing with something equally satisfying. Now, while we discussed target readers earlier in "The Reader: Your Main Squeeze," we should talk more about what a target audience is, and how your chosen genre trope matters to them.

Gotta Hit That Target

I think that sometimes, as writers, it is difficult for us not to get greedy. When we imagine our readers, we imagine a huge mass of innumerable people all shouting praises about our amazing book. But, realistically, most books don't garner that kind of attention or acclaim. Think about it. For every bestselling smash hit, there are haters just waiting to write that one-star review. No matter how popular a book is, it is written for a specific audience, and only the people in that audience will appreciate it. While some may read *Pride and Prejudice and Zombies* by Seth Grahame-Smith and absolutely love every new, unexpected zombie-esque moment, Jane Austen purists look at the cover alone, and gasp as their literary sensibilities are more offended than their noses would be from smelling the decaying zombie flesh portrayed in this adaptation/mashup. The simple truth is that not every book will appeal to every audience, and most writers will never enjoy the benefit of being able to write books that have universal, mass appeal, because most stories just don't work that way. We can't start writing a story and say that our target audience is *every reader.* That's totally unrealistic. Does that mean we should stop trying, stop writing, and run into the doldrums[5]? Of course not. Then, what is a writer *to* do?

Before you start writing the book of your heart, you need to discover who comprises the audience of your heart. Who are *your people* and where can you find them? Do they live under the banner of urban fantasy, coming-of-age, horror, or any other genre of die-hard

---

[5] If you haven't read *The Phantom Tollbooth* by Norton Juster, you really should. It's a pure delight for readers of any age, and has that rare, universal, mass appeal that I described earlier in the paragraph.

fans just waiting for more stories and tropes that will tickle their ears, eyes, and hearts? The difficult truth that writers must understand (at least is was difficult for me to face, maybe you're braver than I am) is that not every book you want to write already has an audience, and creating a new audience for your one story is near impossible to do.

When I first started writing, I wanted to create coming-of-age books that would be written from a Christian worldview (because I couldn't find many, and I wanted them to exist for my daughters to read). But the problem was[6], there wasn't any audience for such a specific type of book. So, all of those books flopped. And by flopped, I mean that they didn't sell. I never got back any of the initial investment I spent on editing or advertising. The biggest mistake I made was that I didn't research anything to determine if a target audience for such a book existed. You might be thinking, "But, wait. You just used *Pride and Prejudice and Zombies* and that seems super specific." And you would be right to bring that up, but the thing is, there *was* an existing target audience for this book.

Editor Jason Rekulak, the man who brought the book idea for *Pride and Prejudice and Zombies* to Seth Grahame-Smith, knew there was a zombie craze going on, and he simply used the huge demand for zombie stories along with the ever-so-dedicated Jane Austen fandom to put out a book that many people didn't realize they already wanted (and without having to acquire any additional rights, because *Pride and Prejudice* was already public domain at that time). I was one of those audience members. Up until two years ago when Claudia Gray's *Star Wars: Lost Stars* made its way onto my reading radar, *Pride and Prejudice* had been my long-

---

[6] Another problem was the fact that these books weren't well-written because I was a newbie writer.

time favorite book. I still read *Pride and Prejudice* every year. But did I know that I would love this story rewritten to accompany the utterly insane theory that the behind-the-scenes going-ons in Meryton in Hertfordshire were motivated by a zombie invasion? Was it on my radar as something I would possibly ever want to read? Absolutely not (truthfully, I don't like zombies all that much). But when it came out, I facepalmed because it was a genius move, and I was sad I hadn't thought of it before editor Jason Rekulak.

So you see, even if your book idea seems crazy, as long as there is a target audience out there that is waiting to read your book (even if they don't know it yet), you will be able to sell your story. But, how do you know whether your story idea has a target audience? You have to research comps (AKA comparables). Comps are books that are in the same genre as your story idea, but having the same genre alone doesn't make another book a comp. If the story idea you have, and the well-selling books you've found in your genre don't have tropes with the same patterns, then your book *isn't* a comp. For example, if you find a book that is a romance where the two enemies become lovers (a popular romance trope), and your book uses the trope of the woman coming back to her hometown to reunite with her teenage love-interest (another popular romance trope) then your book is not a comp to the first book because the tropes are different. Can your book subvert the trope ideas of a comp? Yes. But, these tropes need to have the same steps, big events, or loops. So, is your book a comp of ones that are consistently keeping a high sales ranking? That means the same booming target audience is waiting to buy your kind of story. But remember, you don't write for money, because money can't read books. But you do need a *someone* who wants to read your book, and the best way to find out if that someone exists is to follow the money, and read the reviews.

There are several things I do when I'm researching to see if the new (or super old) book idea I have actually has a target audience, and I'm going to walk you through each step. The first thing I need to decide is if I want to pursue indie or traditional publishing (which is something we cover in the next chapter, so make sure to read that chapter before you decide). Then I need to look for comps. The easiest place to do this for ebooks is on Amazon, because they have lots of very specific categories that I can browse through. If I want to go the indie route, I pay attention to indie books. If I'm thinking about pitching a book to an agent, I look at traditionally published books. If I can find comps that are in the genre I want, with the tropes I want, then I look at the ranking of those books and how long ago they were published. If the top fifty books in that category that fit the trope I'm looking at have an Amazon Best Seller Ranking (ABSR) over 25,000 and were published less than two months before, then I move onto the next step. I use Publisher Rocket to look up the amount of money those books are making. Then I wait a few days and check again. If the books are consistently showing more than $400.00 a month, I know that this genre and trope have lasting demand, and I move forward, planning the book I want to write, while keeping a handy checklist of every part of the trope pattern I need to hit in order to satisfy my target audience's trope desires.

When you're thinking about your target audience, the most important thing you can do is look at reviews of comps, and eventually your own books. Remember that when you choose one audience for your book and story, you are choosing to eliminate other groups of readers, and that's actually what you *want*. But, that means that there will be readers who leave reviews to that effect. This means that you will see bad reviews in your research. You have to be able to dissect them so that you understand whether these reviews are representative of the target audience or not. For example, if an author seems to have written a space fantasy book that is aimed at readers who enjoy adventure stories and you see reviews like "not enough science," you can definitely say that the person who wrote that review is not part of the target audience, they are a part of the science fiction target audience, but that isn't who the author wrote that book for.

Now, this next step takes a bit more practice to employ. You have to be able to look at the reviews for your own books, and understand when a review is a valid piece of usable criticism that can make your next book better, or when it's from someone outside of the book's target audience. For example, when you look at reviews for this book (*Write the Perfect Read- The Fiction Edition*), you will see that there are reviews that call it uninspired, derivative, and basic. You see, they picked up this book hoping to find new and improved writing hacks. While we do have some writing hacks in here and in our other books, the purpose of this book is to take someone who has little knowledge about writing and the writing industry, and give them all of the tools they need in one place so that they can start on their own writing adventure. So, when you look at positive reviews for this book and you see new writers getting so excited about what is written in here, you can see that we have written a book that pleases our target audience. So, we can look at the negative reviews and say, those are okay, and even to be expected. However, if we saw a lot of reviews from new writers who said that our book was confusing and complicated, we would need to reevaluate any future projects written to this target audience.

But, what if the story of my heart, the book I've been waiting to write, doesn't have any kind of target audience? Well, I have two choices. I can decide, based on my market research that there isn't a market for this kind of story right now, and put it on the back burner while I pursue a story that I know has a target audience. Or, I can spend several months planning, writing, and editing this book. Then I can either try to launch it myself (indie) or pitch it to agents (traditional), hoping that I can create a new target market by sharing a compelling story with people that I think will appreciate it. The latter choice leads down a long and winding road that often ends in heartache, but some writers (both writers of this book included) believe that this is a noble journey that some writers must make. But in order to avoid feeling like a total crazy person, I have also decided to write stories that I love, that already have target audiences. This way, I can make some money to fund the books I want to write that I know might not ever make me consistent income. To me, this is a best of both worlds kind of solution. While the choice is the writer's, I wish someone had told me early on that not every story has an audience. I found out the painful way. The tear-filled, empty-walleted way. And now that I know that if one wants to sell a product, there has to be a market for it, I have the option to choose whether I write books that make money or books that mainly feed my individual soul. That knowledge is powerful. And we're sharing it with you.

CHAPTER 11

NOW WHAT?

When I first started writing, editing, and formatting books, this question haunted me. *I have a book that satisfies the desires of my heart, a print-ready PDF, and an .epub[7] file, but now what?* Before I started writing this chapter, I sat, listening to my favorite instrumental playlist and thinking about all of the emotions you must be feeling. If you're petrified, enthralled, or dejected that the book writing process is over, you're in good company. I think that when most writers finish a project and are in the throes of deciding what to do next, they feel a combination of all of these emotions. At least I do, still, after every book. Because each project

---

[7] An .epub file is the main extension for digital book files these days. Even Amazon, which previously only accepted their proprietary .mobi files, now accepts .epub files, so why not just format one file type and be done?

requires a different approach to publication and marketing. In general, we are pro self-publishing because we don't want to share so much of our money with a publisher that will tell us to spend a huge percentage of our advances on marketing for ourselves (don't do that even if they tell you to). However, there are some projects we would consider traditional publishing for. But before we start sorting out all of that, I think it's time to take a moment to celebrate.

<u>You Did It!</u>

Listen, friend (I hope you consider us friends by now because we do). We want you to do something for us. Please pause and say these words to yourself, "You did something amazing that most people only dream about. You've set your mind and schedule to learning how to write a book, and you did it. Think of all the things you sacrificed, time with your loved ones, saying no to doing other fun things, spending your precious brain energy on literally anything else. You are incredible, intelligent, and industrious. Good for you!"

In life, there are moments when we need to reflect on the things we've just completed, but at the same time studies show that when you implement new knowledge (also known as retrieval-based learning[8]), you retain it much better. So don't stop now. Make a plan, find a writing buddy on Twitter (#writingcommunity), get your book plotted, create your character profiles, fill out your setting questionnaire, and start writing your book.

---

[8] For more about this interesting phenomenon, check out an article by Dr. Jeffery D. Parpicke, PhD at https://www.apa.org/science/about/psa/2016/06/learning-memory

Grieving Your Finished Project

Grief is a process we all go through when we face the end of something in our lives. It can be a relationship (due to death or separation), a project, or a season. Writing is no different. I just finished a five-month update on my first book, *You Aren't Worthless: Unlock the Truth to Godly Confidence.* Though it was difficult, I found the process of taking something my younger writer self had worked on, and polishing it with the skills and acquired knowledge of my older writing self to be quite rewarding. Only now, as I've shifted to this project, have I realized that I will never work on that book again. It was rewritten and planned with all of the knowledge I now possess, implemented in a way that means it is completely finished. It has every tool I know incorporated into it.

Even though I wrote the updated edition of *You Aren't Worthless* with the goal of never having to rewrite or rework any sections again, I didn't realize that when I finished, I would not ever return to this project. And even though I'm relieved it's out there for the world to read and interact with, there is also a remorse that has set in. It's over. This realization and resulting grief are part of a natural process that happens to every writer and creative all over the world. And speaking openly about the grief of moving on to a new project while leaving an old and beloved one behind would benefit the writing community in an intense way. In fact, if you want to contribute to the healing effects of speaking about your end-of-project grief, join us in discussing it on Twitter or Instagram using #creativewritinggrief.

Trad vs. Self-Pub

It is difficult to write a definitive guide about which

publishing path to choose once you've finished your project because the publishing industry itself is constantly changing. However, we can't leave it out simply because of fluctuating industry standards and practices. At the time of this writing, in fall of 2019, these are the most up-to-date approaches to both traditional publishing and self-publishing. Keep in mind that these are succinct descriptions, as we could have written (and many have) entire books about both processes along with something called hybrid authorship, which we will also cover in this section.

<u>Which One Is Better?</u>
That's the question we all have, isn't it? Unfortunately, there is no simple answer to this question. Each of the three ways of publishing has its own distinct advantages and disadvantages depending on your style and genre. Annoying, right? We will examine these pros and cons as we dive into each category. Get your swimming cap.

<u>Traditional Publishing</u>
If the idea of sending an unsolicited manuscript to join the innumerable pile to your favorite editor's desk sounds appealing, you will probably be surprised to know how much traditional publishing has changed over the last ten years. We live in a digital age, so you would think that we can just zip whole manuscripts over to a publishing house for their consideration, but that's not the change that all of our improved technology created. Instead, it is more difficult now than ever to get your manuscript read. With the inundation of ease of sharing, publishing houses have now acquired different strategies and policies to deal with the onslaught of unsolicited manuscripts. If you hope to get your prized pile of papers into the hands of someone who has the power to traditionally publish it,

you must first go through the gatekeeping process of querying to find an agent. But don't worry; though technology has created more barriers for writers, it has also afforded several new means of entry.

Pros

-You control who gets your query, and you can revise each individual cover letter to suit the agent you are querying.

-If your book gets picked up by an agent, they do the publisher shopping for you. They take a percentage of your money, yeah, but they're doing something you aren't allowed to and don't know how to do. Money well spent.

-Once you sign a contract, you get $$$$. Woot, yay for advances ya'll.

-The publishing house pays for the cover design, formatting, and your ISBN identification number. In some cases they also pay for developmental and copyediting, but that differs by house.

-If your book does well, you have the potential for maximum exposure. Those publishing guys know lots about marketing, and they already have reader trust.

-They set up speaking engagements and book tours for you. Shrug off that burdensome planning and pack your bags.

-If your book sales exceed their expectations you might get a reprint and a contract for your next (still unwritten) book.

-Rinse and repeat with the same agent, who has a vested interest in your success.

Cons

–Your manuscript will be confined to industry standards in terms of word count and reader expectations dependent on your genre.

–You have to query. This process can take a long, long time, and requires you to temper your own rejection.

–Your agent might not be able to sell your book to publishers. This usually equates to the end of your professional relationship.

–If you get a contract, the publisher expects you to spend almost all of your advance on marketing, which you probably don't know how to do (also, don't do this). They might also make you pay for your editing out of your advance.

–If your book does well, you have already signed away the rights and your publishing house is taking a HUGE percentage of all the profits that come from your book.

–You don't get a say in who your developmental editors or copyeditors are. You don't get to pick your own cover. You sign away your digital rights when the publishing company doesn't incur any extra costs to create an ebook version of your book aside from initial .epub formatting. You cannot control any of your own marketing or promotions. The book goes on sale when they say it does.

–If your print books don't sell, the book stores that agreed to purchase them can sell them back to the publisher at any time (like, forever) and *you* will have to pay them back out of your advance.

I will add one more pro to this list: if you ever want to write books for a favorite fandom (I wouldn't say no to a deal from Del Rey Books), you must go traditional.

Self-Publishing AKA Indie

For the purpose of full disclosure, we want to point out that this book—the one you are currently reading—was produced via self-publishing. We love this process and tend to prefer it to traditional publishing. But you should do whatever fits your writing goals. There are several major disclaimers for indies that trad pub authors don't have to deal with, but I'll leave those for the list. Indie (short for independent) authors existed long before the creation of Amazon. These writing pioneers would create and photocopy their own books—complete with cover and binding—and distribute and sell them to friends and fellow readers. This was before you could press a 'compile' button and have a print-ready PDF stored neatly on your computer.

As technology increased, people who couldn't or didn't want to embark on the journey to traditional publishing found that they could sell their books online. Amazon allowed these authors to have a platform beginning with their AmazonEncore program in 2009, and soon other companies started to follow their lead. Now self-publishing has turned into a booming industry that has numerous hard-hitters and even traditional publishing companies looking to compete. In 2015, Macmillan Publishers tried their own self-publishing platform, Pronoun, but for reasons we won't suppose, they shut down new submissions in 2017 and closed permanently in 2018. But why are so many people suddenly interested? There is a huge market for book services and indie publication where millions of dollars are up for grabs. Every time I sell one of my books through Amazon, they get a chunk of the profits, but in their Amazonian wisdom, they take less than a traditional publisher would. However, as you will see in the following pro/con list, the amount of work an indie author has to keep track of and pay for can intimidate even the most passionate DIYer.

Pros

–The power is yours! With complete creative control, you can make every single decision on your own.

–Self-publishing offers you the option to buck genre word count standards and reader expectations (but you have to be careful about both).

–You get to decide which book service professionals to work with.

–You get to market your own book according to your own goals and budget.

–Your intellectual property stays yours, and you can do whatever you want with it (including using backlist books to create book sets for more effective marketing).

–You get to keep way more of the profits (there is no con for this point, and it is the one that most decisions to go indie hinge upon).

–Branding is easier. When you have total creative control, that means you can make all of your books have a distinct *look* to them so that when members of your fan base see your books, they recognize them as yours instantly. If you are traditionally published, each book or series is probably going to look completely different. Traditional publishers don't necessarily care about marketing you as an author because they are too busy branding your books for a specific genre. When you are self-published, you can brand and rebrand without a third party's restrictions.

Cons

-You *have* to make every decision about your project, and that requires copious research so that you can stay up to date on industry trends and standards. Even though your book is self-published, that doesn't mean your competition will be. That means you have to keep your book knowledge current.

-You have to find all of your own book services professionals and vet them. You also have to pay them for everything they do out of your own pocket. Because of this one item on the list, you must understand how every part of the book creation process works so that you can communicate effectively with each professional you hire.

-Writing and marketing are extremely different. Now you have to learn a new skill set. And be careful, because you can throw away thousands of dollars paying for marketing that doesn't work.

-You have to pay for and set up your own ISBN identification numbers... well, you should. Amazon, Nook, Ingram Spark, and other companies offer to let you use an ISBN they assign for free, but you can't use any of those across multiple platforms and you won't be able to get your book into any libraries with any of those numbers.

Hybrid Authorship: Choose Your Own Adventure

The great thing about being a hybrid author is that you can mix and match both traditional and indie publishing in order to chase after different goals. Maybe you have a book that you know would be a great fit for trad pub, but you have a separate series that would shine in self-publishing. Do both. Just remember that once you have signed away the rights to one of your stories, that's it until that contract is up. Make sure you read everything carefully, and hire a literary lawyer to help you be sure that you know what you're signing.

Our current recommendation for self-published authors that are getting courted by trad pubbers is to try to keep your digital rights. If you can work out a deal where you only sell the print rights, that's your best bet. Right now deals like that are rare, but if you're doing so great without the big publishing house backing you, consider how long their offer would provide you with income compared to your current self-published-generated monthly income. A great example of knowing when to hold is Hal Elrod, who turned down an offer for traditional publishing for his book *The Miracle Morning: The Not-So-Obvious Secret Guaranteed to Transform Your Life (Before 8AM)* but accepted representation for his new book *The Miracle Equation: The Two Decisions That Move Your Biggest Goals from Possible, to Probable, to Inevitable.*

Don't Panic

Though an initial read-through of these lists might feel intimidating, the thing to know is that with any of these lists, you can create systems that will help you as your career progresses. If you choose to go down the trad pub path, you can build a great team comprised of your agent, editor, and publisher. If you want to try the indie route, you can find awesome professionals and build your own team of designers, editors, advanced readers (people who read your book before you publish it), and marketing experts. Remember, any worthwhile endeavor takes time and effort; writing is no different.

Audio What Now?

Adding audio to a novel isn't something everyone thinks of doing while writing. Publishing the book can be enough of a nightmare, who needs more drama? But let me make my case first before you skip to the next section.

I don't think it will come as a surprise to you, but I love reading. Learning how to read was one of my greatest accomplishments. Nothing bad could come out of it. At least that's what I thought originally. Well, as it turns out, something bad did happen. My mom stopped reading to me so often. Before that, I used to follow her around the house, carrying a selection of my favorite fairytales, trying to catch her in between tasks so she could sit and read to me. Turns out, that wasn't as much fun for her as it was for me. Boy, did I love being read to. My mom knew it. I knew it. She thought I liked the stories, but I think I also liked spending that precious time with her, having her all to myself (I am the youngest of three, so that was a pretty big deal for me). Well, audiobooks haven't actually made up for all those read-out-loud sessions, but it's comforting to know that someone has taken the time to read me an entire novel, which I then can listen to again and again, absolutely guilt-free.

Audiobooks aren't just for people who want to speed through their to-be-read pile while driving to work. They're not just for the artists who enjoy a good novel while painting or sewing. They're not just for the lone joggers who can't find the time to read at home. Audiobooks are also for the visually-impaired, who no longer have to wait for books to be adapted into braille. They're for the dyslectic, to whom reading causes extreme fatigue and frustration. They're for the foreigner who wants to be exposed to the new language as much as possible and model proper speech delivery.

Have I convinced you that audiobooks are a good idea yet? If yes, keep reading.

The single most important thing that can make or break an audiobook is the narrator. Stephen King narrated a few of his novels, and I can't help but admit that I felt closer to him as a writer. I mean, come on, Stephen King himself read for me! What better way to enjoy the story than hear it straight from the same man who created it?

Being able to narrate your own novel is surely an asset. However, if you are microphone shy and would rather hire someone, do some careful research first, and what better way than to listen to some of the best-selling books that fall under the genre you're writing in. Here's what you'll be paying attention to. You don't want a narrator who speaks in monotone. Chances are your audiobook listener will lose interest. Or, maybe they won't have the opportunity to lose interest because they won't bother buying your audiobook in the first place (don't forget that certain book-selling sites offer free audio samples). Imagine the repercussions of causing drowsiness to a driver. You don't want that on your conscience. No, your narrator has to be able to use the proper intonation that fits your material, which is what you would have done if you had narrated it yourself.

That's why you need to collaborate with someone who has read and understood the soul of your work. The safest bet is to hire a voice actor as your narrator. Voice actors are trained to explore their material and give a lively delivery. These amazing people can play the entire cast of a novel. A talented voice actor will change register, accent, and gender in such a way to make the listener forget the story is being narrated by a single person. Trust me, finding the right person to do the narration will do your work justice and take your readers on the wonderful journey you intended for them to have.

When you look at your text as a script for an audiobook narrator, something happens. Your perspective changes. If you make each chapter into a script for your narrator (which is what you should do), you will start to notice that maybe not all of the things you wrote are as concise or clear as you imagined. The "read out loud" test will help you understand if you have communicated successfully, and it will also give you an idea of how the narrator you've selected (if you aren't performing the book yourself) will be able to interact with the listeners. It is also important to watch for words that you could change to make the listening experience more encompassing. For example, where you have "Now that you've read," you could change to "Now that you've listened to…" or "Think back to what you read" can be changed to "Think about what you heard me say in the last chapter." The best thing about preparing your book for audio narration is that you will catch any tiny mistakes that didn't get caught in editing, and you will know whether your words have the impact and meaning you dreamed they would have. Plus, having the audiobook option for your audience expands your brand and gives you an added layer of legitimacy in the reader's eyes (or in this case, ears).

A Final Note On Querying

We mentioned that querying is a necessary step in the

traditional publishing journey, but what is querying? In regards to finding an agent, a query is a document you create to pitch your novel while including all of the pertinent information. It usually includes all of the juicy tidbits of your protagonist mixed into a plot and hook salad, topped with a few facts about your word count, genre, and comparables. In regards to working with a developmental editor or copyeditor, a query is a question that they have asked you (the author) in order for clarification to repair a confusing, inconsistent, or erroneous passage, phrase, or word.

Again, if you want to understand how to write a query to submit in order to find representation through an agent, we suggest you go read through Query Shark, queryshark.blogspot.com, all of it. If you want a free and easy place to pitch, go to Twitter and look up when the next #PitMad event will be. Remember, during #PitMad only agents are supposed to like tweets they want to represent, but if you see something you would want to read, retweet it. For more information on this amazing technological phenomenon, simply search for "pitmad" in your favorite search engine (I used to try to link to different resources about this topic, but the websites kept disappearing).

Let's Review

No, not *that* kind of review. In this section, we need to talk about the reader review. It is the single most important piece of marketing you have for your book. This is especially true if you are self-publishing, because Amazon and its cohorts base everything off of your book reviews. We're not going to get into the nitty gritty of how to deal with negative reviews here (whatever you do, don't respond) because that is kind of far away from where you are right now. What we do want to talk about is how you cannot expect your family or friends to review your book. First, it's against Amazon's terms for KDP authors. Second, your family and friends are probably not your target audience.

Save yourself from tears and frustration by beginning your writing career under the assumption that most people *will not* be supportive. You're doing something that sounds hard and crazy to people who don't understand how rewarding writing can be. If you have a supportive group that rallies around your book and career, great, but that isn't the norm for most writers starting out. Find solace among your fellow writers and work hard to get reviews from people that *are* your target audience. Twitter is a great place to start.

CHAPTER 12

THE END

A Note From The Literary Symmetry Team

We want to start out the final chapter by saying, "Thank you!" We appreciate that you took the time to read our carefully compiled and information-rich book. Hopefully your brain doesn't hurt too badly. Remember, the best way for you to retain what you learned is to use it as soon as possible. And we want to support that endeavor. Post a picture of your project (or you working on project) on Instagram with the hashtag #writetheperfectread and we'll feature a few of these posts on our account as they come in.

Before you go, can you do us a big favor? Would you go leave us a review for this book on the online book retailer of your choice? We choose to work as indie authors, and that means that reviews are extremely important to us.

By now, you've realized that we both work as editors for Kristin's editing co-op, Literary Symmetry. Our goal is to help authors create perfectly symmetrical manuscripts at affordable rates. Let us be a part of your writing business's systems. We want to help you give birth to a fully matured book-baby. If you've read this entire book, you understand how passionate we are about effective storytelling. Check out our website to schedule your editing time-slot today at https://literarysymmetry.com/services/

In addition, if you want to find out more about the plethora of tips and tricks involved in successful storytelling, we are launching an online school that will take you from not knowing how to write, to being able to write and sell or pitch your first novel, with all of the information, coaching, and support you need in 2021. Head to academyofstorytelling.com to get on our mailing list for updates and fun and free writing goodies.

Do You Like Free Stuff?

If you like things that are free, good, because we have a free online course that will teach you how to stop doing the one thing that readers hate most. Imagine how much better of a chance you would have to get more positive reviews and win readers over if you could stop doing the one thing that drives them crazy. Head on over to literarysymmetry.com/storyfilters to get started with your free PDF, walk-through video, and audio book today. We know you are going to *love* this resource (and your readers will love the end result once you implement it).

And for free writing advice, book and film reviews, and her fiction writer's workshop, you can check out Kristin's podcast *Expensive Words* on various podcast platforms or at expensivewords.com.

Recommended Resources For Further Learning

As we're sure you noticed, we like to read and watch a ton of stuff to keep our knowledge base forever expanding. Here are few books and films we recommend to stretch your storytelling muscles.

The McGraw-Hill Education Handbook of English Grammar & Usage (Third Edition) by Mark Lester and Larry Beason—a wonderful mishmash of grammar implementation with a touch of humor, this book is a great overall usage guide that will help you to eliminate some of your most egregious grammar errors.

The Sense of Style: The Thinking Person's Guide to Writing in the 21st Century by Steven Pinker—though this book is written mainly from a descriptivist standpoint (to understand what descriptivist and prescriptivist thinking entail, you can listen to Episode 2 of Kristin's podcast *Expensive Words* titled "The Two Types of Grammar Advice") it is still an immeasurable resource that will help you understand why grammar is so important, and which "writing rules" aren't really rules at all.

Story Engineering by Larry Brooks—this quick read will take you through the main processes we described as far as plot points, but a bit more in-depth. Though we don't agree with his *Lovely Bones* obsession, we both found this book helpful at the beginning of our writing careers.

The Shawshank Redemption (the film)—though this film definitely has some mature content (trigger warning: one of the topics of this film is rape), it is a modern masterpiece in storytelling. Next time you watch this gem, take notes on the ways that the character development and timeline are set up.

On Writing Well by William Zinsser—this perennial bestseller was originally written for nonfiction writers, but there is plenty of outstanding information in this book for every writer. Just remember to take everything with a grain of salt. Our advice would be to largely ignore Zinsser's admonition to abandon reflexive pronouns.

Yes, You Can

Although writers will often poke fun at people who say "I'd write a book, too, if I ever found the time," as if it's some easy feat to accomplish, the truth is that it does take time. But that doesn't mean it's impossible. Both of us work full-time jobs, and we make the time to write, just like you probably do. We believe in you, and if you ever need some extra cheerleading, just tweet us @LiterarySymmet1 with your tweet #peptalk and we'll send you a personalized pep-talk. You've got this, and we're here to help.

Don't Forget

If you haven't already, don't forget your free set of printable worksheets about character, setting, and plot. As a bonus, you'll also be signed up for our helpful emails, that alert you about our newest products, service sales, and give you an opportunity to get our next book free as an advanced reader copy (ARC). Head on over to https://literarysymmetry.com/wtpr-f/ to download your free worksheets, now.

REFERENCES

Books

Jane Austen, *Pride and Prejudice* (New York: Penguin Publishing Group, 2002).

Claudia Gray, *Star Wars: Lost Stars* (California: Lucasfilm Press, 2017).

Karen Hesse, *Phoenix Rising* (New York: Square Fish, 1994).

James Schannep, *Click Your Poison* Series (James Schannep, 2012).

Judy Blume, *In the Unlikely Event* (New York: Penguin Random House, 2015).

Kristin N. Spencer, *Decisions & Desires* Series (Sincerely Adorned Books, 2016).

Kristin N. Spencer, *Plunge Into Darkness* (Sincerely Adorned Books, 2018).

James S. A. Corey, *The Expanse* Series (New York: Orbit, 2011).

David Bayles & Ted Orland, *Art & Fear: Observations on the Perils (and Rewards) or Artmaking* (David Bayles, 1993).

James Clear, *Atomic Habits* (New York: Avery, 2018).

Darren Hardy, *The Compound Effect* (Pennsylvania: Vanguard Press, 2010).

Brian P. Moran, *The 12 Week Year Field Guide: Get More Done In 12 Weeks Than Others Do In 12 Months* (New Jersey: John Wiley & Sons, Inc., 2018).

Shawn Achor, *The Happiness Advantage: how a Positive Brain Fuels Success in Work and Life* (New York: Currency, 2010).

William Strunk Jr., *The Elements of Style, Fourth Edition* (Pearson, 2019).

Stephen King, *Carrie* (New York: Anchor Books, 1974).

Ernest Cline, *Ready Player One* (New York: Broadway

Books, 2011).

Kristin N. Spencer, *Gaze at the Stars* (Unpublished, 2018).

Hal Elrod, *The Miracle Morning: The Not-So-Obvious Secret Guaranteed to Transform Your Life (Before 8AM)* (Hal Elrod International, Inc., 2017).

Hal Elrod, *The Miracle Equation: The Two Decisions That Move Your Biggest Goals from Possible, to Probable, to Inevitable* (New York: Harmony Books, 2019).

Mark Lester & Larry Beason, *The McGraw-Hill Education Handbook of English Grammar & Usage, 3rd Edition* (McGraw Hill Education, 2019).

Larry Brooks, *Story Engineering* (Ohio: Writer's Digest Books, 2011).

William Zinsser, *On Writing Well: The Classic Guide to Writing Nonfiction, 30th Anniversary Edition* (New York: HarperCollins, [1976] 2006).

Donald O. Hebb, *The Organization of Behavior: A Neuropsychological Theory* (New Jersey: Laurence Erlbaum Associates, 2002).

Websites

Christopher Bergland, "Reading Fiction Improves Brain Connectivity and Function." 2014. *Psychology Today.* https://www.psychologytoday.com/us/blog/the-athletes-way/201401/reading-fiction-improves-brain-connectivity-and-function.

Pew Research Center, "The Rise of E-Reading Part 2: The general reading habits of Americans." 2012. *Pew Research Center Internet & Technology.* https://www.pewresearch.org/internet/2012/04/04/part-2-the-general-reading-habits-of-americans/.

Multiple Authors. Writing with Color. *Tumblr.* 2020. http://writingwithcolor.tumblr.com.

Jeffrey D. Karpicke, "A powerful way to improve

learning and memory." 2016. *American Psychological Association.* https://www.apa.org/science/about/psa/2016/06/learning-memory.

Television
   Paul Attanasio & David Shore, *House, M.D.* (2004–2012).
   Jeff Lindsay, *Dexter* (2006–2013).
   Fox Studios, *X-Men: The Animated Series* (1992-1997).
   Ronald D. Moore, *Battle Star Galactica* (2004-2010).

Film
   Tim Burton, *Batman* (1989)
   Guillermo del Toro, *Hellboy & Hellboy II: The Golden Army* (2004, 2008).
   Anna Boden, Ryan Fleck, & Geneva Robertson-Dworet, *Captain Marvel* (2019)
   Ruben Fleischer, *Venom* (2018)
   Michael Caton-Jones, *Doc Hollywood* (1991)
   Barry Sonnenfeld, *For Love or Money* (1993)
   Stephen Spielberg, *Jurassic Park* (1993)
   Richard Marquand, *Star Wars: Episode VI–Return of the Jedi* (1983)
   Frank Darabont, *The Shawshank Redemption* (1994)

Authors Mentioned (in General)
   Henry David Thoreau
   Joseph Conrad
   Rachel Hauck
   Margaret Atwood
   Zig Ziglar
   Dan Brown
   Mark Twain
   Malcom Gladwell
   Charlie N. Holmberg

James Patterson

ACKNOWLEDGEMENTS

From Maria...

A great thank you to my partner-in-crime, Kristin, for inspiring me and cheering me on throughout the whole process of writing this book. I still can't believe you never gave up on me. Watching you put this book together was an educational journey. Your help has been so immeasurable that 26 letters are not enough for me to write how much I owe to you. And, hey, thanks for honoring me with your precious friendship. I love you.

Thank you to my close friends who have been there to support me, each in their own unique way. I'll pay you back for all the tissues, I promise.

Another thank you to my family who have put up with so many of my crazy schemes and new ideas I come up with every two seconds. One of these days, you guys, one of these days...

Thank you, Vasiliki, for being the most amazing goddaughter a godmother could have asked for. Having someone like you looking up to me is one of the greatest gifts I'll ever get. I love you and can't wait for you to grow up a little more and read this book on your own.

Thank you to all those YouTubers who have uploaded hour-long videos of relaxing fireplace sounds, and the Forest app guys who have helped me stay as focused as I could be.

One last thank you to my adorable, mixed-breed, black-and-white dog, Cora (short for Corazon), for keeping my feet warm during the writing of this book. You're my heart. Thanks for making me a better human.

From Kristin...

Thank you first to Maria, who went along with this

crazy scheme to write a book together while being over 5,000 miles (around 8,000 kilometers) apart. I appreciate all of the late nights, tears, and time you poured into this project. I know it's going to help people write amazing stories. I couldn't have done it without you (really). I love you. Also, I appreciate you letting me pick the house style. I know that wasn't easy. Two stubborn women who both work as editors writing together about writing, what could go wrong? But seriously, I am so proud of you. Thank you for putting up with my "boss mode."

Thanks to Travis (AKA Mr. Cute Face), my kids, and my two fluffy puppies, for tolerating copious amounts of random stops in conversation when I had to take a call or text about this book. I love you guys. There are no words that can capture how much I love you. Your support is everything.

To Aunt April, thank you for being so understanding and working our schedule around my meetings. I love and appreciate you more than you'll ever know. Also, thank you for the writing fuel (snickerdoodles).

Thanks, Mom, for all of your support via text messages and phone calls from several thousand miles away, as always. Love you!

Thank you, Jess, for all of the Panera-located conversations about what makes a writer. You are a great friend and wonderful writer. I can't wait for your novel to reach the world.

Thanks, Denise, with whom I had countless conversations about this book. Your friendship and industry experience are both priceless to me.

Thank you to the Greensburg Writing Group. A lot of the thoughts in this book were borne out of our conversations around the table at the art museum. I'm so glad I found you, and now that this project is over, hopefully I can finally attend more meetings.

The biggest thanks to my absolute favorite, Jesus. Your peace really does pass all understanding.

ABOUT THE AUTHORS

Maria Mountokalaki is a teacher, copyeditor, translator, and full time mom to a black and white dog named Cora. Her expertise is in the area of teaching English as a second language, which is also the type of Master's degree she holds. When she isn't doing any of those scholarly things, you can find her playing (and reviewing) board games, DnD, walking in the woods with Cora, or enjoying her homemade pizza with her friends. Her passion for nonfiction is unparalleled, and her loyalty to her friends is unmatched. For more writing by Maria, check out her blog *Did I Just Write This* at https://didijustwritethis.wordpress.com Maria currently resides in Athens, Greece.

Kristin N. Spencer is a bestselling author, a certified copyeditor, a developmental editor, and a mom to three kids. She hopes to inspire her children to follow their dreams by doing so herself, running the editing co-op Literary Symmetry, playing Dean of Story Magic at the Academy of Storytelling, and writing several books a year, some fiction, some nonfiction. She is married to bestselling author and founder of Neighborhood MakerSpace, T.E. Spencer, who would have the manliest beard in the world if it didn't bother Kristin so much when he lets it grow wild. They all live together in a super nerdy house in

Western Pennsylvania with two dogs, Spartacus and Mooncake. For more writing by Kristin, check out her website at https://confidentnobody.com or check out her podcast at https://expensivewords.com.

STORY FILTERS

What if you could learn to stop doing the one thing readers hate most? How would that change your writing? Head on over to

 https://literarysymmetry.com/storyfilters

to take the totally free course, *Story Filters*, that teaches you to stop doing the one thing readers can't stand. *Story Filters* will teach you how to employ easy-to-use story filters that will transform your writing forever. Don't wait until you start writing your next project, learn how to use story filters now, and for free!

Printed in Great Britain
by Amazon

23826043R00101